# MICRO FICTION

# Writing 100-Word Stories (Drabbles) For Magazines and Contests

## A Self Study Tutorial

## Michael A. Kechula

BooksForABuck.com
2014

BooksForABuck.com

2014

ISBN: 978-1-60215-276-2

# About Writing

Getting published and winning contests are based on a number of unpredictable factors which are out of the author's and publisher's control and are associated with the vagaries of the publishing industry. The author and publisher can't guarantee that readers of this book will ever get a drabble published, or win a drabble-writing contest even after learning and applying all the techniques in this book. Further, because of individual learning differences, the author and publisher can't guarantee that readers will be able to comprehend and implement everything contained in this book.

# ACKNOWLEDGEMENT

This book is dedicated to my life-long guide and illuminator, THG, and to the late Dr. B. F. Skinner, Psychologist and Harvard Professor. Dr. Skinner's extraordinary book, "The Technology of Teaching," profoundly changed the author's life.

# MENU

# INTRODUCTION

Are you eager to get published in magazines as quickly and often as possible? One way to do that is to learn how to write 100-word micro-fiction stories called *drabbles*. There's a continuing demand for them by editors of online and print magazines. Besides that, writing contests that specialize in drabbles are held regularly. Why not exploit the demand by developing and submitting some drabbles?

Perhaps you've never tried to write such tiny tales, and don't know how to craft them. One way to learn is to review all the topics in this book and complete all the exercises.

Here are some things to know about this book:

- It's a self-study tutorial designed to teach you how to write genre fiction drabbles that tell complete stories.
- It was written by an author who developed self-study books and online distance-learning courses for the IBM Corporation and other Fortune 500 companies.
- It was written after the author analyzed and critiqued hundreds of drabbles written by his students and others. The contents are based on a minimalist approach the author developed to transform dozens of novelists and short story writers into drabble authors.
- It contains 9 chapters consisting of 76 topics, 425 examples, and 165 drill and practice questions.
- It includes a Word Economy Exercise consisting of 125 questions
- It presents examples of drabbles that won contests and were published in magazines.

Chapters and topics vary in size, depending on their level of complexity. We suggest you repeat any topic any number of times until you feel you've mastered the contents.

As you proceed through the chapters, we'll present some information, show examples, then ask questions about what you just read. All questions begin with **Q** followed by a number. If you have the eBook version, have a pencil and plenty of paper available to answer the questions. If you have the paperback version, write your answers in this book.

Answers for all questions within each chapter are available at the end of the chapter. Answers for the Word Reduction Exercise are at the end of that exercise.

Most questions are drill-and-practice exercises to reinforce what you just learned. They allow you to monitor your progress in absorbing the tutorials and putting them into practice. The ultimate goal is to prepare you to develop drabbles that will attract the attention of magazine and contest editors.

If you're ready to learn how to write drabbles the minimalist way, let's get started...

# CHAPTER 1: DRABBLE BASICS

This chapter covers the following topics:

- **Definition of Drabble**
- **Characteristics of Literary Drabbles**
- **Characteristics of Genre Drabbles**
- **Characteristics of Anecdotal Drabbles**

## DEFINITION OF DRABBLE

A drabble is a complete story that's told in exactly 100 words, not counting the title. A drabble is the only form of fictional story-telling prose that has such an exact, rigid, and enforced word requirement.

Q1: What is the allowable word count for a drabble? _____

Q2: A story containing exactly 100-words is called a _____.

Some authors erroneously think the word drabble is just a new name for a vignette. However, three notable differences distinguish drabbles from vignettes:

- Drabbles tell complete stories, but vignettes don't.
- Drabbles are restricted to precisely 100 words, but vignettes can have as many words as an author wishes.
- Drabbles take several hours to develop, but vignettes can be developed as fast as you can enter words into a word processor.

Q3: Name one of the differences between drabbles and vignettes. _____
_____

Magazines and contest editors seek 2 kinds of drabbles:

- Literary
- Genre

Let's take a look at the characteristics of literary drabbles…

## CHARACTERISTICS OF LITERARY DRABBLES

Literary drabbles tend to be lyrical, focus on characters and have little or no plots.

Q4: Literary drabbles focus on characters, don't have extensive plots, and tend to be _____.

Q5: Literary drabbles tend to focus on_____.

Here's an example of the opening sentence for a literary drabble:

*I always thought naming girls after flowers was antiquated and ridiculous, but as I lay here, watching her sleep, I stroke the alabaster skin of her shoulder and think that perhaps this once, the comparison is appropriate.*

Notice how this 37-word sentence focuses exclusively on a character. The remaining 63 words showed even more about the character, and didn't include a plot.

Although a number of magazines seek only literary drabbles, this book doesn't discuss how to develop them. The focus here is on genre drabbles, because they are in far greater demand by contest and magazine editors, world-wide.

Now that we've discussed some characteristics of literary drabbles, let's move on to genre drabbles…

## CHARACTERISTICS OF GENRE DRABBLES

Genre drabbles are considered the opposite of literary drabbles, because they don't focus on characters. Instead, they focus on events, plus they have developed plots.

Q6: Genre drabbles have plots and focus on _____.

By *events*, we mean the noteworthy things that happen in a story. For example, if you're telling about a man who's on his way to a bank to rob it, you'll probably focus on what happens when he arrives. You wouldn't expend words describing his motivations, what he wore, and the color of his hair. Instead, you'd establish the fact that someone wanted to rob a bank, tell what happened when he arrived at the bank, and if he succeeded or not.

Most stories published today are works of genre fiction. Here's a partial list of genre names:

- Adventure
- Crime
- Fantasy
- Gothic
- Humor
- Mystery
- Religious
- Romance
- Science Fiction
- Thriller
- War
- Western

This list isn't complete, but it's large enough to help you understand how genre fiction stories are classified. To learn more about fiction genres, search Google with these keywords: *fiction genres.*

Q7: List 4 of the genre fiction names we just showed you.

Each genre is divided into one or more subgenres. For example, searching Google, we found a list of 31 subgenres for fantasy. Two of them were urban fantasy and magical realism.

Q8: Each genre is divided into one or more _____.

Q9: Name one of the fantasy subgenres we mentioned above.

By now you should be aware that there are two kinds of drabbles: literary and genre.

Genre drabbles are divided into 2 kinds:

- Those with a protagonist and antagonist.
- Those without an antagonist.

A protagonist is the main character of a genre drabble, who wants to attain a particular goal. An example of a goal is to rob a bank. In contrast, an antagonist is a character who tries to prevent the protagonist from achieving his goal. This clash creates conflict and tends to make drabbles more interesting. At the end of the drabble, the protagonist either succeeds or fails to attain his goal.

Q10: What's the role of an antagonist in a genre drabble?

Q11: A protagonist is the _____ _____ of a story.

Q12: Which of the following is true about antagonists?

    a.  They help protagonists achieve their goals.
    b.  They try to prevent protagonists from achieving their goals.


Antagonists are not limited to people. Protagonists may face resistance from other sources such as: animals, inanimate objects, monsters, nature, society, space aliens, supernatural, and even their own psyches.

Genre drabbles that don't have antagonists are called *anecdotal drabbles*.

## CHARACTERISTICS OF ANECDOTAL DRABBLES

Anecdotal drabbles don't have an antagonist. No antagonist = no conflict. But that doesn't mean lack of conflict has to result in a dull story. With careful crafting, anecdotal drabbles can tell interesting, thought-provoking, and amusing tales.

The protagonist's goal in anecdotal stories can be ordinary or extraordinary. An example of an ordinary goal is when someone wants to go to Disneyland to have fun. It's considered an ordinary goal, because everybody would like to go to Disneyland to have fun.

Examples of two extraordinary goals are when a protagonist wants to build a time machine, or capture a Martian.

In anecdotal drabbles, antagonists never show up to prevent protagonists from having fun at Disneyland, building a time machine, or capturing a Martian. Thus, protagonists always achieve their goals without any interference.

Q13: Suppose a drabble tells us Lisa's goal is go to a bakery to buy jelly donuts. She does that without any problems. Is this an anecdotal drabble?


Q14: Suppose in a drabble Harry's goal is the same as Lisa's. Before he reaches the bakery, he's kidnapped and held for ransom. Antagonists have prevented him from attaining his goal. Is this an anecdotal drabble?


We'll now show you three of our published drabbles to illustrate what was just covered. The first example, "Charlie's Amazing Beach Towel," is a genre drabble that includes an antagonist.

The second example, "Reducing Crime," is an anecdotal drabble. This drabble has two protagonists who have an extraordinary goal.

The third example "Back Home at War's End," is also anecdotal, which means it has no antagonist. In this story, the protagonist has an ordinary goal.

Here's the first example…

**GENRE DRABBLE WITH ANTAGONIST**

*CHARLIE'S AMAZING BEACH TOWEL.*

*Charlie invented a shark-repellent beach towel. Dipping it in chicken soup, he wrapped it around himself, and jumped into the ocean.*

*Two great whites raced toward him. Spotting the towel, they screeched and swam away. Their carcasses were found floating on the surface. Autopsies indicated they'd been scared to death.*

*CNN broadcasted Charlie's second test. Billions witnessed sharks fleeing from Charlie while he was wrapped in his amazing towel.*

*Next day, CNN broadcasted Charlie's funeral.*

*Nobody knew Loch Ness Monsters considered beach towels dipped in chicken soup gourmet treats, and that they'd swim thousands of miles just to eat one.*

Q15: Who was the protagonist in the story you just read?

Q16: Who was the antagonist in this fantasy drabble?

The next story has two protagonists who have an extraordinary goal. We wrote this drabble to meet editor guidelines that said we had to include the words *three moons* somewhere in the story.

## ANECDOTAL DRABBLE WITH EXTRAORDINARY GOAL

### *REDUCING CRIME*

*"Police say crime jumps 95% during full moons," Bill said. "By eliminating our three moons, we can reduce crime."*

*"How can we remove three moons?" Joe asked.*

*"Find genies who grant wishes."*

*They advertised. A genie responded. They explained their noble goals.*

*"Mighty big order," the genie said. "Those moons are massive."*

*"Does that matter?"*

*"Sure. If I remove them, the entire cosmos may collapse."*

*"If that happens, could we restore everything with another wish?"*

*"Yes."*

*"Let's proceed."*

*They made their wish. The genie granted it. The moons disappeared.*

*KABOOM! The cosmos collapsed.*

*Unfortunately, nobody survived to wish it back.*

In the fantasy tale you just read, the protagonists achieved their goal. However, the result was disastrous for the entire Universe.

Let's look at the third example…

## ANECDOTAL DRABBLE WITH ORDINAY GOAL

### *BACK HOME AT WAR'S END*

*America was heavily nuked during World War Seven.*

*When the war finally ended, the Army pulled us out of Oceana and sent us home.*

*The first day back, Sarah and I strolled along desert sands at the edge of the ocean. Don't get too close to the water," she said. "It's still highly radioactive."*

*"It's the same way in Oceana," I said. "I can't get over how different everything looks around here."*

*"Yes. It's heartbreaking. Those nuclear missiles that hit us were terribly destructive."*

*"Still, it's wonderful to be back in Las Vegas, watching the sunrise over the Atlantic Ocean."*

The story you just read is an anecdotal drabble of the fantasy genre in which a protagonist had an ordinary goal: to be home and have a normal life. However, to make the drabble more interesting, we included the horrible idea that nuclear war was waged, and the US was a target. The kicker in the final sentence gives the impression that the nation was so severely impacted, Las Vegas now borders the Atlantic Ocean. This implies over 2,000 miles of the eastern United States no longer exists. Notice how we combined fantasy and elements of horror, and provided a twist at the end.

This concludes the Chapter 1. The next chapter discusses the steps of the drabble development process.

## ANSWERS TO QUESTIONS

Q1: 100
Q2: Drabble
Q3: Any of these:
- Drabbles tell complete stories, but vignettes don't.
- Drabbles are restricted to precisely 100 words, but vignettes can have as many words as an author wishes.

- Drabbles take several hours to develop, but vignettes can be developed as fast as you can enter words into a word processor.

Q4: Lyrical

Q5: Characters

Q6: Events

Q7: Any 4 of the following that we mentioned: Adventure, Crime, Fantasy, Gothic, Humor, Mystery, Religious, Romance, Science Fiction, Thriller, War, Western.

Q8: Subgenres

Q9: Magical realism or urban fantasy

Q10: They prevent protagonists from achieving their goals.

Q11. Main character

Q12: Item b: They try to prevent protagonists from achieving their goals.

Q13: Yes

Q14: No. It's a genre drabble.

Q15: Charlie

Q16: Loch Ness Monsters

# CHAPTER 2: DRABBLE DEVELOPMENT PROCESS

The drabble development process has nine steps:

- **Step 1: Decide What to Write.**
- **Step 2: Use Minimalist Approach**
- **Step 3: Create 1$^{st}$ Draft**
- **Step 4: Count Words**
- **Step 5: Read Drabble**
- **Step 6: Edit Drabble**
- **Step 7: Repeat Steps 4 through 6**
- **Step 8. Check Spelling**
- **Step 9: Count Words in Final Draft**

Let's look at the first step…

## STEP 1: DECIDE WHAT TO WRITE

This step involves three tasks:

- Read magazine or contest guidelines.
- Decide to submit a drabble that meets the guidelines.
- Come up with a story idea to meet the guidelines.

Magazine and contest guidelines will give you a starting point by providing one or more of the following:

- A general statement of what editors seek, such as zombie stories.
- A specific word prompt, which can consist of any number of words. Sometimes the words of the prompt must be included in the story.
- A photo showing concrete or abstract images.

Suppose a magazine's guidelines give this word prompt: *blood*. Now you have to come up with a story that refers to blood in some way. You may think of hospitals, vampires, war wounds, stabbings, or any number of things relating to blood.

However, if nothing comes to mind that appeals to you, or if you draw a blank, try this little exercise. It can be done with pen and paper, but a voice recorder is better. Here's what to do: say the word *blood* slowly ten times. You'll find thoughts coming forth very quickly. Write them on paper as fast as you can, or speak them into the recorder without censoring anything. You may find that you suddenly get several story ideas.

Let's assume you now have a story in mind, and are ready to proceed to the next step…

## STEP 2: USE MINIMALIST APPROACH

The minimalist approach we've devised for drabble development consists of these objectives: *to tell as much story as possible, in as few words as possible, without sacrificing a smooth read.*

Q1: What are the objectives of the minimalist approach for developing drabbles?

To meet these objectives, you should strive to use word economy in every sentence of the story. That means you'll have to examine your sentences very carefully to determine which details are essential to describe an event, and which are trivial.

Q2: To meet minimalist objectives you must strive to use _____ _____ in every sentence of your drabble.

Here's an example. Say you wrote this opening sentence for a drabble: *On a bright and sunny day in October, six-foot tall Charlie Smith, a man known to dress exceedingly well, went to a bank with a loaded pistol.*

Let's identify essential details and trivial details, and list them.

ESSENTIAL DETAILS: *Charlie went to a bank with a loaded pistol.*

TRIVIAL DETAILS:

- *On a bright sunny day* (weather report)
- *in October (*date*)*
- *six-foot tall* (character's height)
- *Smith* (character's last name )
- *a man known to dress exceedingly well* (how Charlie dresses)

Why are the weather report, date, character's height, character's last name, and his dressing habits trivial details? Because they have nothing to do with the event of Charlie going to a bank with a loaded pistol. These details merely add useless and needless filler to the sentence. Even worse, they waste precious word count that could be put to better use in developing the plot.

Further, if trivial details weren't separated from essential details, this opener would consume 27 words. That's 27% of the total word count available for the entire story. Only 73 words would be left to tell the rest of the story.

Q3: To ensure that you've included word economy in every sentence of your drabble, you should examine each sentence for _____ details and _____ details.

Q4: How would you define a trivial detail in a drabble sentence?

Q5: List the trivial details in this sentence: *On a bright and sunny day in October, six-foot tall Charlie Smith, a man known to dress exceedingly well, went to a bank with a loaded pistol.*

Q6: How many words containing essential details are in this sentence? *On a bright and sunny day in October, six-foot tall Charlie Smith, a man known to dress exceedingly well, went to a bank with a loaded pistol.*

Let's look at another opening sentence. *"I just saw a Martian at Wal-mart," Susan said, as she scratched her nose.*

ESSENTIAL DETAILS: *"I just saw a Martian at Wal-mart," Susan said.*
TRIVIAL DETAILS: *as she scratched her nose*

Susan reported an interesting event through dialogue. Every word she said was essential. However what she did with her body while speaking is a trivial detail. Scratching a nose while talking in a drabble is an insignificant body movement that distracts and adds nothing of value to the event or plot.

Deleting the trivial detail *as she scratched her nose* frees up 5 words that can be put to better use elsewhere in the story. This doesn't mean that those exact words should be inserted somewhere else in the story. This is what we mean: when you cut five words from a sentence, you gain five word count to compose the rest of your story.

One way to understand word count is to visualize an imaginary word bank. Let's say the word bank consists of a box filled with 100 blank wooden tiles. When you want to create a drabble, the first thing you'll do is withdraw some tiles, say, 14 of them to compose an opening sentence. On each blank tile you withdraw, you'll write one word and any associated punctuation using a marking pen. After you write a word on a tile, lay it on a table, until all 14 tiles are in sequence. Now you read the entire sentence you created by writing words on tiles.

Since you used 14 tiles for the opening sentence, you still have 86 blank tiles left in your word bank to develop the rest of your drabble.

Let's say you wrote these 14 words and punctuation on 14 tiles now resting on the table: *"I just saw a Martian at Wal-mart," Susan said, as she scratched her nose.*

While reading this opening sentence you recall what you learned about essential and trivial details from this book. When you examine the words on the 14 tiles on the table, you notice five tiles contain these words of a trivial detail: *as she scratched her nose.* To remove the trivial detail, you pick up the five tiles and return them to your imaginary word bank.

When tiles are returned to the word bank, the words written on them magically disappear. A quick count of all blank tiles now in the bank shows you have 91 to compose the rest of your story. Thus, by eliminating a trivial detail, you gained five word count that can be put to better use in the story.

The nine tiles still on on the table contain these words and punctuation: *"I just saw a Martian at Wal-mart," Susan said.* You'll let these nine tiles remain on the table, because they contain nine words of essential details, plus they provide an intriguing opening sentence.

Now you withdraw more blank tiles from the word bank to compose the second sentence. As before, you write a word and its associated punctuation on each tile, then lay the tiles on the table. As you go through this imaginary sequence for every sentence, you'll notice words that can be removed. Before your story is complete, you'll find yourself removing tiles from the bank and returning tiles numerous times.

Since you don't actually have a word bank with blank tiles to keep score, the easiest way to keep track of how much word count expended at any given time is to use the word count feature of your word processor. The word processor, in essence, becomes your word bank. You'll type words into a file, examine them, delete them, invoke a word counter, then repeat that sequence until you have a polished 100-word tale that's ready to submit to magazines or contests.

Since word count is so critical for drabbles, we mention it extensively throughout this book in hundreds of examples. To save space from this point forward, we'll use the abbreviation WC to mean word count.

Q7: Although we just introduced you to the idea of essential and trivial details in drabbles, see if you can identify what's essential in this sentence: *Hunched over, hands stuffed in pockets, they ambled down the winding path.*

Q8: How many words of trivial details did you find in the sentence shown above?_____

Q9: List the trivial words you found when examining the sentence in Q7.

Q10: Let's say you included this sentence in the first draft of your drabble. *"I have terrible dreams about vampires every night," Lisa said, shifting her weight in the uncomfortable chair.*
How would you rewrite it to remove trivial details?

Q11: By cutting trivial details in the sentence shown above, how much WC will you free up to use elsewhere in the drabble?

Q12: Find the trivial details in this sentence, remove them, and rewrite the sentence. *She cupped her chin in a tiny fist and stared solemnly at the computer screen.*

Here's something else to consider after you identify trivial details in a sentence and remove them. Sometimes the remaining essential details will still contain more words than necessary. The only way to tell for sure is to examine the essential details for additional deletions. Let's look at an example to see how that works.

ORIGINAL SENTENCE: *Nick, a guy who loved pizza more than anybody he knew, was the first person to lay his eyes on the crashed UFO.*

ESSENTIAL DETAILS: *Nick was the first to lay his eyes on the crashed UFO.*

TRIVIAL DETAILS:

- *a guy* (Nick's name implies he's a guy. No need to remind readers of that fact.)
- *who loved pizza more than anybody he knew* (Nick's food preferences)
- *person* (The name Nick already implies he's a person.)

Removing trivial details, you end up with: *Nick was the first to lay his eyes on the crashed UFO.*

When we examine the essential details again to see if we can achieve even greater word economy, we notice some inflated prose. By that we mean too many words are used to describe something. This is shown in the example below:

WITH INFLATED PROSE: *Nick was the first to lay his eyes on the crashed UFO.*
WITHOUT INFLATED PROSE: *Nick was the first to see the crashed UFO.*

The inflated prose in the sentence is *lay his eyes on.* It's a wordy way of saying *see.* Both mean the same thing. Substituting *see* for *lay his eyes on,* allows you to cut 3 WC. You can confirm this by counting the words in both sentences.

Although the result is a perfectly good sentence, a bit of rewrite can remove even more words.

BEFORE: *Nick was the first to see the crashed UFO.*
AFTER: *Nick saw the crashed UFO first.*
BEFORE WC: 9
AFTER WC: 6
GAINED WC: 3

Note that in the illustration above, BEFORE WC = the WC of the original sentence before we changed it. AFTER WC = the WC after we made the change. If you subtract AFTER WC from BEFORE WC you'll see how much WC was gained. Gained WC should always be used to the fullest advantage, so you can tell as much story as possible in as few words as possible.

Let's look again at the original sentence about Nick and the UFO, and the final, rewritten sentence:

BEFORE: *Nick, a guy who loved pizza more than anybody he knew, was the first person to lay his eyes on the crashed UFO.*
AFTER: *Nick saw the crashed UFO first.*
BEFORE WC: 23
AFTER WC: 6
GAINED WC: 17

What began as 23-word sentence has been condensed to a 6-word sentence, without changing the essential details. This is the essence of word economy that allows you to tell as much story as possible in as few words as possible. Notice that the final sentence remains a smooth read, which meets minimalist objectives.

The original sentence had 23 WC. 100 WC available for the drabble minus 23 WC used for opening sentence =77 WC remaining to tell the rest of the story. Through careful editing we cut a total of 17 WC. Adding the 17 WC gained to the 77 already available gives a new total of 94 WC to tell the rest of the story.

Not all word cutting is as extensive as this example. Sometimes you'll find that you can spot only one word to delete in a sentence, such as: *the, that, and.* Deleting one WC still contributes toward your efforts in achieving word economy in a drabble.

Here's a note of precaution when you cut words from a sentence. Sometimes when cutting too much, the results can make the sentence choppy and unclear. To determine if you've cut too much, ask yourself the following questions for each word you've eliminated:

- Is this word necessary to advance the story, enhance dialogue, or strengthen the plot?
- Will my story become less comprehensible if I remove the word?
- Does the sentence sound too choppy after I remove the word?

You can determine how smoothly a sentence is after cutting words by reading aloud the original version and the changed version. Keep the sentence that sounds best.

Let's take a few moments to review the steps we took in this exercise to achieve the maximum amount of word economy.

- We began with this 23-word sentence: *Nick, a guy who loved pizza more than anybody he knew, was the first person to lay his eyes on the crashed UFO.*
- We determined which words contained essential details and which contained trivial details.
- We deleted the trivial and ended up with these essential details: *Nick was the first to lay his eyes on the crashed UFO.*
- We examined the sentence further and discovered it contained inflated prose: *lay his eyes on.*
- We substituted the word *see* for *lay his eyes on.*
- We realized that the remaining essential details could still be cut by a bit of rewrite. That gave us this sentence: *Nick saw the crashed UFO first.*
- We achieved word economy by reducing a 23-word sentence to a 6-word sentence. We did this without

changing the meaning and without sacrificing a smooth read.

Examining your drafts to determine what's essential, what's trivial, and if there's any inflated prose are just three techniques for achieving word economy and minimalist objectives. There are dozens more detailed in Chapters 4 through 8 of this book. All help you work toward the goal of telling as much story as possible, in as few words as possible, without sacrificing a smooth read.

Here's another example of inflated prose: *I learned how to read when I was five years old.*

We can cut three WC without changing the meaning: *how, years, old.* After deleting those words, the sentence becomes: *I learned to read when I was five.* The BEFORE and AFTER illustration is shown below:

BEFORE: *I learned how to read when I was five years old.*
AFTER: *I learned to read when I was five.*
BEFORE WC: 11
AFTER WC: 8
GAINED WC: 3

Let's move on to Step 3 of the drabble development process…

## STEP 3: CREATE FIRST DRAFT

This occurs when you convert your thoughts into words and enter the words into a computer file.

While you're doing this, don't be overly concerned about the number of words you compose in your first draft. Nobody writes a perfect 100-word drabble on the first try. Most writers exceed 100 words the first time around.

## STEP 4: COUNT WORDS

Use your word processor to count the words in your draft. Take note of that number, because it points to how many words must be cut. Your goal is to tell a complete story in 100 words.

Note the following, which could result in a miscount when using your word processor counting feature:

- Hyphenated words count as one word. Example: well-written counts as 1 word. So does 5-million. However, do a spell check to ensure your hyphenated words are valid.
- Words preceded or followed by an ellipsis count as 1 word each. Here's an example:
  *"I...feel...sick."* Some word processing programs will count this string of three words as only one word. To get the correct WC, remove the ellipsis between each character, run the WC program, and reinsert the ellipses before submitting your drabble.
- Don't count the dash after a space as one word, it's merely punctuation. For example: *"I'm as real as —"* I *broke off, realizing the stupidity of what I'd started to say.* Some word processing programs will count this as a 17-word sentence. However, counting by hand shows it's actually a 16-word sentence.
- Any keyboard symbol preceded and followed by a space may be counted as one word. Examples are * % ( ) $. Therefore, if you are showing dollar amounts in your story, ensure you don't put a space between $ and the amount. See the examples below:

  COUNTS AS 1 WORD: $100
  COUNTS AS 2 WORDS: $ 100
  COUNTS AS 1 WORD: ($100)
  COUNTS AS 2 WORDS: ( $100)
  COUNTS AS 3 WORDS: ( $100 )

Considering the above, run some experiments to see how your word processor handles the items listed. This way, you'll know how to avoid miscounts when preparing your draft.

## STEP 5: READ DRABBLE

Here's where you read your draft. We suggest you read it aloud. There's a noticeable difference between reading you story out loud and reading it silently.

As you read, ask yourself these questions:

- Did the opening grab attention?
- Did the narrative sound smooth?
- Did transitions from one paragraph to another use minimum WC?
- Did transitions sound smooth?
- Did the dialogue sound smooth?
- Did the dialogue sound realistic for the situation?
- Was the dialogue pertinent?
- Were there any trivial details in the dialogue?
- Was the dialogue crisp?
- Was every sentence clear?
- Did everything make sense?
- Were there any trivial details in the narrative?
- Did some narrative phrases or sentences seem unnecessary?
- Did something in the narrative sound awkward?
- Were some words, especially pronouns, repeated excessively within a sentence or paragraph?
- Were there any points at which you had to stop the recorder to ponder the meaning of a word, phrase, sentence, or piece of dialogue?
- Did the voice sound the way you intended?
- Did the story fully represent what you intended to tell?

- Did you use word economy everywhere possible?
- Did you tell as much story as possible with as few words as possible?

**STEP 6: EDIT DRABBLE**

Editing your first draft means recognizing needed changes and making them. Start by cutting trivial details and inflated prose from every sentence. Next, apply any of the 57 other word-cutting techniques detailed in Chapters 4 through 8. The topics within those chapters are listed below:

**CHAPTER 4: Developing Minimalist Openers**
> Hooks
> Quick Set Up
> Changing the Subject
> Weather Reports
> Trivial Details
> Cryptic Sentences
> Inflated Prose

**CHAPTER 5: Developing Minimalist Characters**
> Last Names
> Complicated Names
> Repetition of Titles
> Clothing
> Facial Expressions
> Watching, Glancing, Glaring
> Turning
> Body Movements
> Sighs
> Smiles
> Nods
> Head Shakes
> Shrugs
> Cookbook Procedures
> Impossible Mannerisms
> Pauses

    Cryptic Sentences
    Obscure Words

Let's move on to the next step of the development process…

## STEP 7: REPEAT STEPS 4 THROUGH 6

This is usually the most dynamic and intense step of the development process. You'll find yourself deleting words, adding words, juggling WC, and rewriting sentences numerous times until you feel you've developed a polished drabble that's ready for submission.

As you work on your manuscript, we suggest you keep all the iterations and versions in a single file. This way you'll have a complete record of everything you wrote for a drabble, from beginning to end.

The amount of time you'll spend doing this is unpredictable. We've spent up to four hours repeating steps 4 through 6 for a single drabble. We think the payoff is worth the effort every time we win a contest or receive an acceptance from a magazine editor.

## STEP 8: CHECK SPELLING

Use your word processor's spell check program to spot misspellings. Fix all spelling errors.

As an extra precaution, consult a dictionary when homonyms appear in your manuscript. For example, if you meant to say *the wind blew*, but wrote *the wind blue*, the spell check program won't catch this error. The same could happen with some contractions. For example, if you meant to write *"I like your coat,"* but you entered: *"I like you're coat,"* the spell check program won't catch the error.

## STEP 9: COUNT WORDS IN FINAL DRAFT

Use the WC feature of your word processer to ensure the final draft of your drabble contains exactly 100 words, not counting the title. Ensure you don't have a miscount, if your draft contains symbols that are preceded and followed by spaces.

This concludes Chapter 2. The next chapter discusses what you should consider before you begin the drabble development process.

## ANSWERS TO QUESTIONS

Q1: To tell as much story as possible, in as few words as possible, without sacrificing a smooth read.
Q2: Word economy
Q3: Essential and trivial
Q4: Trivial details have nothing to do with an event. They add useless and needless filler to the sentence.
Q5:

- On a bright sunny day
- October
- six-foot tall
- Smith
- man known to dress exceedingly well

Q6: 9
Q7: They ambled down the path.
Q8: 7
Q9: Hunched over, hands stuffed in pockets, winding
Q10: "I have terrible dreams about vampires every night," Lisa said.
Q11: 7
Q12: She stared at the computer screen. It can't possibly matter to the plot of a drabble what she did with her chin, or how she stared at a computer screen.

# CHAPTER 3: BEFORE YOU BEGIN

This section covers the following subjects:

- **Be a Storyteller**
- **Tell, Not Show**
- **Make Stories Event-Driven**
- **Avoid Mundane Plots**
- **Write Clear Sentences**
- **Include Dialogue**

## BE A STORYTELLER

When you develop drabbles for magazines or contests, we suggest you think of yourself as a storyteller first, then a writer second. We've seen hundreds of drabbles that displayed the opposite. Consequently, they were often mundane and without plots.

If you're not sure how to develop your drabble as a storyteller, we suggest you write the story using the same words you'd use when telling it to a friend over coffee. For example, suppose you want to tell your friend about a party you went to last night. Would you tell him like this? *"I went to a great party last night while the stars shone brightly in the sky and the moon gave off just enough light to give the ground a wondrous, silvery patina."* Or would you say this? *"I went to a great party last night."*

Hopefully, you'd use the words shown in the second example. That's the storyteller's way of relating a story, while the first sentence is the writer's artful way of embellishing a sentence with lots of visuals. You can't help but notice the startling differences between the two.

Let's say you now want to tell your friend you met a gorgeous woman at the party. Would you tell him with these words? *"I met a gorgeous woman at the party with golden treads cascading over her shoulders, and falling gently on her very stylish, expensive-looking, silk dress."* Or would you say this? *"I met a gorgeous woman at the party."*

Once again we see the differences between both ways of relating the story. One is direct and to the point using word economy, and the other is loaded with trivial details your friend won't care about. In fact, if you continued to speak in such a round-about way, your friend might become impatient and ask you cut all the fluff and get to the point. That's exactly what we're asking you to do when you develop drabbles. The best way to accomplish that is to adopt the minimalist approach which is to tell as much story as possible in as few words as possible, without sacrificing a smooth read. By now you should know that means using word economy in every sentence.

## TELL, NOT SHOW

Writing drabbles the minimalist way means you'll have to place far more emphasis on telling than showing in the narrative. Showing is a neat option when you have plenty of WC available to tell a story. But with drabbles, you're limited to exactly 100 words.

Showing becomes an impediment to drabble development, because more words are needed to show than tell. For example, if we want to show that a male character is well-dressed, we could burn up quite a bit of WC describing his outfit from top to bottom, including colors, fabrics, and names of high-fashion designers on garment tags. Authors might expend dozens of words just to portray a very simple idea: a man was well-dressed. In contrast, only four words are expended by telling the reader *the man was well-dressed,* considering *well-dressed* counts as one word.

The emphasis on telling in drabbles doesn't mean you'll have to give up showing entirely. You'll still be able to show some things about characters through carefully crafted dialogue.

Q1: Which approach is preferable when developing a minimalist drabble, showing or telling?

Q2: Why is telling preferable to showing when developing drabbles?

Q3: _____ can be used in drabbles to show some things about characters.

## MAKE STORIES EVENT-DRIVEN

Event-driven stories require far less WC than character-driven stories. If you're not sure of the differences between them, consider the following:

- In event-driven stories, *events* take precedence.
- In character-driven stories, *characters* take precedence.

Q4: Because of WC limitations, drabbles are _____-driven.

Q5: In an event-driven story, _____ take precedence.

Here's an example of one of our published drabbles that is event driven...

## BILLY'S QUEST

*Governor Jones visited an orphanage and asked children, "Whadda ya wanna be someday?"*

*"A pizza," Billy said.*

*"Why?"*

*"Nobody loves me. But everybody loves pizza."*

*"He's a lunatic! Abandon him in the forest."*

*"What are you?" asked a chipmunk.*

*"A boy," said Billy. "But I wanna be a pizza so somebody will love me."*

*Chipmunk mumbled magic words.*

*Billy became a pizza.*

*Chipmunk hollered to relatives, "Look what I have."*

*"Wow! Pizza!" they yelled.*

*Between burps, 50 chipmunks proclaimed their powerful love for pizza.*

*When a girl chipmunk chewed the last morsel with razor-sharp teeth, Billy proclaimed, "I'm finally loved."*

## AVOID MUNDANE PLOTS

Some magazines publish drabbles with ordinary plots that diminish their entertainment value. The story you just read has a plot that's hardly ordinary. That's why we often choose fantasy when creating genre drabbles.

Another way to avoid mundane plots is to including a twist in your drabbles. We can tell you from experience, this isn't an easy task.

To give you an idea of how we approached this problem, we'll show you a few examples. Let's begin with one of our published drabbles. We wrote this one in response to the prompt *whale,* issued by the moderator of a writing group.

Mulling over the prompt, we came up with the idea of somebody saving whales in a satirical and absurdist way. We also hoped to include a twist. Here's what we ended up with, after 4 hours of writing, editing, and juggling WC:

### *SAVING THE WHALES*

*Harry was whale watching. Suddenly, a whale came to the surface and cried out, "Save us, Harry."*

*"How?"*

*"We're starving for caramel flavored popcorn."*

*Harry told UN environmentalists about his intention to save the world's whales. Applauding his compassion, they agreed.*

*Harry bought 1,000,000 tons of caramel flavored popcorn. He charted 100 gigantic ships to dump it into the world's oceans.*

*The whales were so delighted, they named Harry their first President. Time Magazine declared him Man of the Year.*

*Then, whales got morbidly obese, high blood pressure, diabetes, strokes. Soon, all died.*

*Harry joined the list of assassinated presidents.*

Just because we selected the fantasy genre for this drabble doesn't mean other genres won't work. It's a question of whether or not you can dream up a concept for, say, a crime tale in response to the *whale* prompt that can work and have a twist in so few words.

We said earlier this drabble took 4 hours to develop. In contrast, we knew an author who claimed he'd developed a polished drabble in just 20 minutes. He'd done this prior to becoming our student. When reading his story, we found what we suspected: a clearly written collection of words that had no plot. What he'd actually written was an extremely short vignette, but not a complete story.

Any author who can develop a compelling, publishable drabble in 20 minutes that has a twist and meets minimalist objectives is a literary genius.

## WRITE CLEAR SENTENCES

Always write as clearly as possible. To do otherwise could doom your work and guarantee rejection by contest and magazine editors.

We've seen quite a bit of murky and cryptic writing in drabbles. We've never understood why authors waste time and effort writing that way.

Here are some examples of murky sentences we found distracting. Each time we encountered cryptic writing, we were thrown out of the story.

- *He was always filling the space I was in, and then leaving it suddenly, leaving me teetering on the edge of the space he had just encroached.*
- *She listened as old age skulked, muttering, into a corner.*

- *The world reveals itself to me as a viscous, richly colored liquid. I glide through, but am not part of it as it whips and snaps like a dragon's tail.*
- *His heart pounded, as a warm breeze whispered over parts of his body that had never been privy to nature's breath.*
- *They wallowed in universal access to his works, reading not Terms and Conditions.*
- *Charlie knew the judge didn't just say what he thought he said.*
- *Blood-red neon outside makes liquid demands.*
- *He yawns and gives it a five-count.*
- *She squidged her toes into a bereft stiletto and hobbled to a step.*

Ensure you always write as clearly as possible. If you aren't sure you've succeeded, ask someone to read your drabble to see if they understand it.

## INCLUDE DIALOGUE

Dialogue can make drabbles more exciting and dramatic. But there's a more important reason for including it: well-crafted dialogue usually consumes less WC than narrative.

To illustrate this, let's look at the first draft of a drabble we wrote. Like most first drafts when composing drabbles, it ended up with more than 100 words. In fact, this one has 159 words, and contains only narrative. We did several rewrites, but found we couldn't reduce it to 100 words. When switching to dialogue, we were able to achieve our goal.

First we'll show you the first draft that contained only narrative, and then we'll show you the dialogue version that got published.

NARRATIVE VERSION – FIRST DRAFT

## A BENEVOLENT DECISION

*Liz had a bad accident and ended up in a hospital. She was in a coma for 3 years. When she woke from the coma, a doctor was at her bedside. She asked where she was. He told her she was in General Hospital.*

*When Liz asked what happened he told her she'd fallen off a high cliff, and that it caused her to be in a coma for 3 years.*

*She said her head felt odd and asked for a mirror. The doctor wouldn't give her one. When she asked him why, he said she needed therapy first. She thought that meant something horrible might have happened to her face. He said her face was fine.*

*The doctor told her things had changed while she was in the coma. When she asked what things, he told her the Supreme Court had made a benevolent decision. When she asked what decision, he said the one that allowed head transplants.*

DIALOGUE VERSION – FINAL DRAFT

## A BENEVOLENT DECISION

*"Where am I?" Liz asked.*

*"Central Hospital," said Dr. Brown.*

*"What happened?"*

*"You fell off a high cliff. You've been in a coma three years."*

*"Why does my head feel so odd?"*

*"You'll get used to it."*

*"Gimme a mirror."*

*"Not now."*

*"Why?"*

*"You need therapy first."*

*"Oh No! Did something happen to my face?"*

*"The face is fine."*

*"Why did you say 'the face?' Gimme a mirror now, or I'll sue!"*

*"Calm yourself. Things have changed."*

*"What things?"*

*"The Supreme Court made a wise and benevolent decision. It saved your life."*

*"What decision?"*

*"The one allowing head transplants."*

Q6: Which of the following is true about dialogue in drabbles?
  a. Well-crafted dialogue uses fewer words than narrative.
  b. Every drabble must include dialogue, or editors will reject it.

This concludes Chapter 3. The next chapter discusses the minimalist way of creating opening sentences for your drabbles.

## ANSWERS TO QUESTIONS

Q1: Telling
Q2: Telling uses fewer words than showing.
Q3: Dialogue
Q4: Event-driven.
Q5: Events.
Q6: a. Well-crafted dialogue uses fewer words than narrative.

# CHAPTER 4: MINIMALIST OPENERS

This chapter discusses how to enhance a drabble's opening sentences, and how to meet minimalist objectives when composing openers.

Include the following to enhance opening sentences:

- **Hooks**
- **Quick Setup**

Omit the following to meet minimalist objectives when composing openers:

- **Changing the Subject**
- **Weather Reports**
- **Trivial Details**
- **Cryptic Sentences**
- **Inflated Prose**

Let's look at the first topic and how it can impact your drabbles…

## HOOKS

Try to include a hook in your opening sentence that will grab the attention of editors and make them want to continue reading. This is often a difficult task for many authors no matter what is a story's length. It becomes even more challenging when developing drabbles.

Your drabble's opening sentence should also bring editors into the story instantly and give a clear idea of what the story's about. Here's an example from one of our published drabbles:

*Madame Majestic's price to resurrect Harold's dead girlfriend was $1,000 and the tip of his thumb.*

If you were a magazine or contest editor, would you want to read more about Madame Majestic, Harold, and his dead girlfriend? Does this opener give you a strong clue of what this story's about?

Look at this drabble opener: *Icy crystals pelted Howard's face, just as his ex-girlfriend's icy words had pelted his heart.*

- Did this opening sentence about icy crystals grab your interest?
- Did the sentence give you a clear idea of what the story is about?

Turned out, the story that opened with icy crystals pelting a character's face was about the protagonist meeting an ugly woman in a bar. Consequently, using words to describe what icy crystals did to the protagonist's face was completely unrelated to the tale and should've been deleted. Since only 100 words are available to tell about meeting someone in a bar, a better way to approach the opener would be to place the protagonist in the bar and tell what his goal is. One possible example: *When my girlfriend jilted me, I went to a bar to find somebody new.*

Exercise: Copy the sentence above in the space below. Use it as an opening sentence for a drabble. What would you write for the next sentence? Take as much time as you need to consider this. When you get an idea, write it below the opener.

Here's another example of a drabble's opening sentence that gives no clue about the plot: *We had prepared for this for a very long time.*

When we read this sentence, we wondered what the characters had prepared for. The author could've told us by substituting appropriate words for *this*, such as *war, famine, plague, wedding, picnic, alien invasion.* However, we didn't find out until the story's last sentence that the characters had prepared for an attack by children. We never learned why the children were going to attack, how they were going attack, or if the attack ever occurred.

Exercise: Copy this opening sentence below: *We were prepared for a Martian attack.* What would you write for the next sentence? When you get an idea, write it below the opening sentence.

Exercise: Suppose you're a magazine editor who's about to read submissions for next month's issue. Below is a list of opening sentences extracted from drabbles. As you read each opener, see if it grabs your interest, or makes you yawn. Then, ask yourself if the opener gives you a good idea of the drabble's plot.

- *I followed them to the stadium.*
- *The exhaust from our thermal packs clouded into mist.*
- *Charlie switched on the TV.*
- *The virus spread across the planet causing a total breakdown of society.*
- *I was in line at the canteen excited about this new gravy chicken roll that was being offered on the menu.*
- *Helen opened a beauty parlor.*
- *Day 1: Catastrophic engine failure.*
- *They don't pay me enough to do this job.*
- *"Dear Mother," he wrote.*
- *Trenton gazed at the sky, grinning.*

- *After burying the seed, Neria stood and stepped back, letting the moons bathe the ground in silvery light.*
- *I bought my daughter guppies to apologize for inviting the plumber who has a crush on her.*
- *"Do I have to go in today?" Jonathan asked while pulling up his pants and sliding out of bed.*
- *One minute before midnight, the inmate began to scream for his life.*
- *It was a windy October day.*
- *Benny cranked up his radio.*
- *"What do you think we'll find on the dark side of the Moon?" Harry asked.*
- *"It's a secluded place, over two-thousand square feet, with a fully finished basement."*
- *Their eyes locked and the rest of the world melted away.*
- *Things moved around her.*
- *Gavin thanked the audience as he accepted the Employee of the Year Award.*
- *"Ladies and Gentlemen," said Dr. Zanker, "we're on the brink of a stupendous scientific discovery."*
- *Four swallows chattered and swooped over the gravel driveway.*
- *The entire surface of Mars was red, except for a ten-foot green rock.*
- *He wasn't mindful of the people around him.*
- *Curious, Frank answered a newspaper ad: "Beautiful Vampire seeks donors."*
- *Sighing, Marcia opened her eyes to greet the new day.*

EXERCISE: For practice, write an opening sentence for a sci-fi drabble.

EXERCISE: For practice, write an opening sentence for a fantasy drabble.

EXERCISE: For practice, write an opening sentence for a horror drabble.

EXERCISE: For practice, write an opening sentence for a crime drabble.

EXERCISE: For practice, write an opening sentence for a humorous drabble.

After you complete the five practice sentences, read each one aloud. As you read each sentence, ask yourself these questions:

- Does the sentence include word economy?
- Is it a smooth read?
- Would it intrigue editors and make them want to read more?
- Would it give editors an idea of what's to come?

If your answer isn't "yes" to every question, rewrite the sentence.

## QUICK SETUP

If you can't devise an opening sentence that gets editors right into the story, try a setup of two or three short sentences.

Here's an example of a two-sentence setup from one of our published drabbles:

*"Where've you been?" asked Marcia.*
*"Monsters kidnapped me."*

The two sentences above used eight words to set up the story. That left 92 more words to develop a fantasy drabble about abduction by monsters.

Here's another from one of our drabbles that has a two-sentence set up:

*Gigantic flying saucers hovered over Earth. Their blinking lights spelled out a warning in every language: REPEAT OR DIE.*

These 19 words set up one of our drabbles that won first prize in a contest.

Here's one of our published drabbles that uses three sentences to create an opener:

*A Martian yelled through a bullhorn, "Attention mall shoppers. Are you disgusted with high gasoline prices? Come to Mars where gas is two cents a gallon."*

Below are set ups that consist of two or three sentences. When you read them, decide if they pull you into the story and give you a good idea of what the story is about. All are extracted from our drabbles that were published in magazines.

EXAMPLE-1:

*Madame Majestic's price to resurrect Harold's dead girlfriend was $1,000 and the tip of his thumb.*

*He agreed.*

*Slicing his thumb, she performed a weird ritual with the bloody flesh.*

EXAMPLE-2:

> *"Ladies and Gentlemen," said Dr. Zanker, "we're on the brink of a stupendous scientific discovery. Tonight, through hypnotic regression, we'll discover exactly how Earth was created."*

EXAMPLE-3:

*Haitian zombies love oatmeal cookies. When discovering Americans spend billions on Halloween treats, they thought that meant oatmeal cookies. Consequently, 125,928 zombies snuck into America to go trick-or-treating.*

EXAMPLE-4:

*I was inspecting the Doomsday Shelter 17 miles below Area 51 when World War 7 happened. Incommunicado, I didn't even know.*

Here are the first two sentences of a drabble that confounded us:

*There.*
*Her.*

Sometimes using a single word in a sentence works to create dramatic impact. However this is not the case with the example you just saw.

Some editors will only read the first two sentences of your drabble. If your work doesn't grab their attention instantly, they'll stop reading. Do all you can to prevent that from happening.

## CHANGING THE SUBJECT

Let's look at another kind of error we've often seen in openers. In this one, the author provided an opening sentence that caught our attention, and then changed the subject in the very next sentence. This caused us to lose interest immediately.

OPENING SENTENCE: *She couldn't put her finger on it but something felt wrong.*
SECOND SENTENCE: *She'd been walking for what seemed like hours, though she couldn't tell for sure.*

The first sentence made us want to know what felt wrong to the character. However, the author chose not to tell us. Instead, the subject was changed immediately to a woman walking for a long time. The next line, not shown here, gave a weather report. At that point, we stopped reading, because the drabble meandered too much.

Here's another:

OPENING SENTENCE: *I came to England when I was seventeen.*
SECOND SENTENCE: *I know what hard work is.*

Notice how the two sentences aren't related to each other in any discernible way. The first gives the idea we'll find out about something involving England and a 17 year old protagonist. The second sentence changes the subject and talks about hard work. Notice how dramatic the second sentence sounds. It would've served as a far better and more impactful opener.

Another example:

OPENING SENTENCE: *It is better when I am alone.*
SECOND SENTENCE: *They say vodka doesn't smell.*

This story meandered quite a bit. Turned out it was a drabble about somebody's mom dying and how her remains were handled. We think it would've been a more dramatic opener if these two words had been used: *Mom died.* The remaining 98 words could then tell how Mom's remains were handled.

Final Example:

OPENING SENTENCE: *"No ice cream!"*
SECOND SENTENCE: *"You're trying to kill me," Jimmy whined.*

For the rest of this 100-word tale, ice cream wasn't mentioned again, nor was any connection made between ice cream and killing somebody.

Let's move onto the next topic…

## WEATHER REPORTS

Don't include weather reports in opening sentences—unless that information is absolutely vital to the plot. We've seen dozens of drabbles that were opened with weather reports. In every instance, the reports were superfluous filler.

EXAMPLE: *The air was cool, but the sun was bright and still carried some summer warmth.*

Turned out that every word in this opening sentence was wasted, because the story had nothing to do with the weather.

Many stories we've read that opened with weather reports suddenly changed the subject in the next sentence. The weather was never mentioned again, making us wonder why it was there in the first place.

If you find it necessary to open with a weather report, ensure it's vital to the plot. An example is when the story is about a major storm. Another is an incident that occurs during a tornado, when the tornado plays a key role in the story. Perhaps you can think of other instances in which weather should be mentioned in the opening sentence.

## TRIVIAL DETAILS

We've seen trivial details in the opening sentences of hundreds of drabbles. None were essential to the plot.

Here's an example of a 33-word opening sentence that includes trivial details: *The subway seat looks clean when Charlie Jones sits down on it, but when he stands up for his stop on 14th, the back of his camelhair coat is almost stuck to it.*

The trivial details are:

- The condition of the seat before Charlie sat on it.
- The character's last name.
- The name of the subway stop.
- What kind of coat the character wore.
- What part of the coat stuck to the seat.

The sentence could've been reduced several different ways. Here's how we rewrote it:

BEFORE: *The subway seat looks clean when Charlie Jones sits down on it, but when he stands up for his stop on 14th, the back of his camelhair coat is almost stuck to it.*
AFTER: *When Charlie tries to get off the subway seat, his coat sticks to it.*
BEFORE WC: 33

AFTER WC: 14
GAINED WC: 19

Here's another example of an opener with trivial details: *After burying the seed, Netia stood and stepped back, letting the moons bathe the ground in their silvery light.*

From the minimalist point of view, the wasted words are:

- *Stood and stepped back*
- *In their silvery*

These seven wasted words account for one third of the WC in the 19-word opening sentence. We think these words should've been deleted.

Q1: Eliminate trivial details and rewrite this opening sentence: *After burying the seed, Netia stood and stepped back, letting the moons bathe the ground in their silvery light.*

Q2: Fix this opening sentence: *Reggie adores penguins, so stiff and proper on land, so gracefully aggressive in water.*

Here's another example of how some authors waste words by including trivial details in opening sentences: *When Rolfe stepped out of the silvery-colored spacecraft, he was the first human to set foot on Mars' uninviting landscape.* The trivial details are: *silvery-colored, uninviting.*

Q3: Rewrite the opening sentence above to cut as many words as possible, including trivial details. HINT: add new words, if necessary. For example, *stepped out of = left* and *set foot = stand.*

Q4: Remove trivial details in this opening sentence: *Judy was startled when an apple hit her head, as she passed under the tree that was loaded with bright red apples.*

Q5: Delete as many words as you can from this opening sentence: *I leaned back against the rigid cushioning of the chair, eager to have the doctor remove the thick, mucus-and blood-encrusted wads of cotton packing that had been shoved into my sinus passages after the surgery.* HINTS: add new words, if necessary. Rearrange the word sequence, if necessary.

## CRYPTIC SENTENCES

When critiquing drabbles, we often saw opening sentences we couldn't comprehend. We were thrown out of the story as we paused to figure out what the authors meant.

Here's an example of a cryptic opener that threw us out of the story: *Madame looked at his face, a mistake.*

After reading this sentence twice, we weren't sure if the author meant it was a mistake to look at the character's face, or if his face itself was a mistake—meaning it may have suffered from failed plastic surgery. Unfortunately, the next sentence changed the subject, so we never found out what the mistake was.

Here's an example of an opening sentence, the meaning of which eluded us: *When I am not awake but thinking about her, Brittany has been painting for ten years.*

More examples of cryptic opening sentences:

- *We were Tuesday and Thursday.*
- *It shoved her ribcage, whirling metal, and her chin flew towards the wheel.*
- *The left hand jealous when the right hand celebrates.*
- *An endless dance, once begun, must proceed throughout eternity.*
- *My name did not touch me today so I waited for the bus with eyes focused in a stare.*
- *Going to the rest room, the reason.*
- *Half an hour, great.*
- *Nuclear winter after the blast, not such a deterrent after its use.*
- *Every evening, pounding the pavements, come rain or shine, with me twenty yards behind.*
- *Once upon a time, there was once.*

We suggest you don't sabotage your story by opening with a sentence that's not comprehensible. This invites rejection by magazine and contest editors.

## INFLATED PROSE

Inflated prose occurs in opening sentences when authors use too many words to tell a simple fact. Look at this example:

BEFORE: *He stirs in the night, holding his breath, listening for the beat of his heart within him.*
AFTER: *He stirs in the night, holding his breath, listening to his heart beat*
BEFORE WC: 17
AFTER WC: 13

GAINED WC: 4

Note how WC is wasted in the BEFORE example to remind us where human hearts are located: *within him.* On the other hand, imagine what an intriguing opener this would have been if the guy's heart wasn't located inside his body, and all that implies.

Q6: Rewrite this opening sentence the minimalist way: *She was already pouring the wine when the planes came in over the water, four black darts silhouetted against a glistening blue.*

Q7: Fix this opening sentence: *They are at dinner at the hotel when they hear the first sound of gunfire.*

Q8: Rewrite this opener: *Percy could enjoy the freedom of having a smoke on his front lawn; so he did.*

This concludes Chapter 4. The next chapter discusses how to achieve word economy for characters.

## ANSWERS TO QUESTIONS

Q1: After burying the seed, Netia let the moons' light bathe the ground.
Q2: Reggie adores penguins.
Q3: Several ways to do this. Here's one way: When Rolf left the spacecraft, he was the first human on Martian soil.
Q4: Several ways to do this. Here's one: Judy was startled when an apple fell from a tree and hit her head. We didn't mention

she was under the tree when it happened. If an apple falls from a tree and hits a character's head, readers will assume the character was near the tree for this to happen.

Q5: Several ways to do this. Here's one: After surgery, I couldn't wait until the doctor removed cotton packing from my sinus passages.

Q6: She poured wine when the planes flew over.

Q7: While dining at the hotel, they heard gunfire.

Q8: Percy smoked on his front lawn.

# CHAPTER 5: MINIMALIST CHARACTERS

This chapter discusses how to meet minimalist objectives for drabble characters. All items listed below should be eliminated to achieve word economy. We tell you why they waste WC and show you how to remove them. We also give you exercise questions to test your ability to eliminate them from your stories.

Here's the list of items to omit when working with characters:

- **Last Names**
- **Complicated Names**
- **Repetition of Titles**
- **Clothing**
- **Facial Expressions**
- **Watching, Glancing, Glaring**
- **Turning**
- **Body Movements**
- **Sighs**
- **Smiles**
- **Nods**
- **Head Shakes**
- **Shrugs**
- **Cookbook Procedures**
- **Impossible Mannerisms**
- **Pauses**
- **Entrances and Exits**
- **Flashbacks**

## LAST NAMES

We've seen hundreds of drabbles in which authors wasted words by including a character's last name. Last names aren't important, unless characters are famous. Every time you cut a last name, you save one WC. The other option is to use only last names and omit first names.

Q1: Why do we suggest you omit characters' last names in drabbles?

Q2: Under what circumstance do we suggest you include a character's last name?

## COMPLICATED NAMES

Don't include first names that are hard to pronounce because of complicated spellings, such as: *Sheiya, Guillaume, Gwendollyne, Alyss.* When *Alyss* is used, the possessive form looks awkward: *Alyss's.* Anything that's awkward doesn't belong in a drabble.

When editors encounter names like this, they may be thrown out of the story as they pause to figure out how they're pronounced.

Sometimes authors try to outdo each other by using cute, trendy names with odd spellings. To ensure this doesn't happen in your story, use simple first names, such as Ann, Barb, Jo, Art, Bill, Dan.

If you decide to assign only last names to characters, ensure you omit complicated spellings such as: *Bourbonne, Kaczmarczyk, de Beurre*.

Q3: Why do we omit last names in drabbles?

Q4: What problem arises for readers when you include a name with a complicated spelling?

## REPETITION OF TITLES

When identifying characters by including their titles in the narrative and dialogue, use titles only once. Afterward, identify characters only by their last names, or substitute a pronoun. This will save WC that could be put to better use. Here's an example in which a character's title is needlessly repeated:

*Highway Patrolman Smith approached Frank's car. "Let me see your license and registration," he said.*

*Frank gave Highway Patrolman Smith both. Highway Patrolman Smith went back to his car and entered Frank's driver's license number into his computer. When he saw the results, Highway Patrolmen Smith pulled his weapon and spoke over the loudspeaker, "Get out of your car slowly and raise your hands."*

Smith's official title appeared four times, which was three times too many. After he was identified by his full title, *Smith* and the pronoun *he* would've sufficed from that point forward. That would've saved two WC each time.

Q5: Fix these sentences: *Dr. John Harlow taught a Psychology course at the university. Charlie Higenlooper decided to take Dr. John Harlow's course. On the first day of class, Charlie Higenlooper went to the room where Dr. Harlow was supposed to teach. Instead of Dr. Harlow, Higenlooper found Dr. Andrea Andrews-Smith sitting at a desk facing the class.*

## CLOTHING

Authors who prefer writing to storytelling often waste words in drabbles by including details of what characters wore. Here's an example: *Lisa wore a white blouse with blue buttons to the dance.*

The only time this information would be vital to plot of a drabble is, say, when a deranged character goes insane when he sees white blouses with blue buttons.

If we drop the trivial details about the blouse and rewrite the sentence we get: *Lisa wore a blouse to the dance.*

Another example: *Charles looked great in his uniform festooned with three rows of battle ribbons.* If we drop details about his uniform, we get: *Charles looked great in his uniform.*

Q6: Rewrite this sentence by cutting trivial details: *Sarah wore black shoes that had a pink band on each side.*

Q7: Make this sentence tighter by eliminating unnecessary words: *The door opened and a man in faded jeans and western shirt walked in.*

## FACIAL EXPRESSIONS

Don't waste words telling us exactly what characters' facial expressions were in any scene.

Here's an example: *Frank's face was flushed when he knocked on Jan's door.*

The action of knocking on a door can stand by itself in a drabble. There's no need for any details about what the character's face looked like while he knocked. This would be okay for novels and short stories where authors need to fill lots of empty space on a page, but has no value when it comes to plot-driven genre drabbles.

Q8: Fix this sentence to conform to minimalist objectives: *"I hate you!" Sally said, noticing how Joe's face turned sour the moment she said those words.*

Q9: Rewrite this one: *Liz looked angry when she said, "I'm very angry with you!"*

Q10: Fix this sentence: *A smile creased his face as he raised his pistol.*

## WACHING, GLANCING, GLARING

We often see reports of characters watching, glancing, or glaring at other characters they've been interacting with in a scene. We find these reports unnecessary, because if characters populate a scene, we figure they must be watching each other to begin with. It's a given—something we don't have to be reminded of.

Here's an example from a drabble: *The two sorcerers glared at each other across a Kansas corn field.*

We considered this report of glaring as an unnecessary break or pause in the story. When characters are glaring, they aren't doing anything active to move the story forward.

This report of sorcerers glaring at each other consumed 12 words, or 12% of the drabble. We would've preferred to read about some action, instead of character's glaring at each other. If the 12 WC had been allocated to the battle scene that ensued, the story would've had far more punch. Turned out the author expended only seven words on the battle scene. Imagine how that scene could've been made more interesting by adding the 12 WC that'd been expended on a superfluous report of characters glaring.

Another example from a drabble: *She smiled at him, then shot him with her Glock 9mm, and watched him crumple to the floor.* Let's examine how we rewrote this sentence:

BEFORE: *She smiled at him, then shot him with her Glock 9mm, and watched him crumple to the floor:*

AFTER: *She shot him, and he fell to the floor.*
BEFORE WC: 18
AFTER WC: 9
GAINED WC: 9

If she smiled at him, she's obviously facing him, so we can assume she sees everything that's going on. Thus, there's no need to tell us she watched him crumple to the floor. We dropped what she did with her face, the brand of pistol, and that it was a 9mm model.

Another example that can be rewritten:

BEFORE: *"Mrs. Perrywinkle," I say, watching as she closes her mouth.*
AFTER: *"Mrs. Perrywinkle," I say.*
BEFORE WC: 10
AFTER WC: 4
GAINED WC: 6

Q11: See what you can do with this sentence: *She glanced at Joe while he shaved.*

Q12: Fix this one: *She saw him throw a rock.*

## TURNING

We've read hundreds of instances where characters had to turn before doing something else in a story. All were superfluous.

For example, in an interesting dialogue stream, suddenly we were told that a character turned to the other to say something.

That gave the impression the characters hadn't been facing each other the entire time they'd been talking, which seemed illogical.

We think the only time a character should turn in a drabble is when it's vital to the plot. For example, a character turned to avoid getting hit by a flying brick. Or, a character turned to avoid getting a bayonet rammed into his chest.

Here's an example of a report of needless turning in a drabble: *We both turned and started back across the field to the car.*

Telling readers two characters had to turn before they crossed a field wastes words. In this case, three were wasted: *both, turned, and.* Further, by substituting *ran* for *started back*, 1 more word can be trimmed. The rewritten sentence can look like this: *We ran across the field to the car.*

Here's another example: *The peddler turned to look at me.*

We didn't understand why the author included this seven-word sentence in the drabble, when the sentences previous to this presented dialogue between a peddler and the protagonist. Since they were speaking to each other for a few sentences, we assumed they'd been facing each other the whole time.

We were surprised when two sentences later in the same story we read another report of turning: *I turned and rushed inside my house.* Thus, 14 WC was wasted in two reports of characters turning. That's almost 15% of the entire story.

Another example: *A plan formed within the beast as it turned to skirt the pond.*

This made us wonder if the plan wouldn't have formed within the beast if it hadn't turned.

This one not only includes unnecessary turning, but also a superfluous body movement, neither of which had anything to do with the plot: *Turning to Bill, she shrugged.* The turn was reported right in the middle of a conversation in which both characters had been facing each other the entire time. Deleting this sentence could have trimmed five WC.

Look at this example:

BEFORE: *Then she turned on her high heels and, slinging her purse over her delicate shoulder, walked out.*
AFTER*: She left.*
BEFORE WC: 17
AFTER WC: 2
GAINED WC: 15

Final example: *She turned and slapped him.* In this case, two people were arguing face-to-face, while trading several lines of dialogue. Consequently, there was no reason for the female to turn before slapping him, because he was already facing her. Removing *turned* plus *and* cuts two WC.

Q13: Fix this sentence: *Just as he turned to leave, the streetlight flickered.*

Q14: Rewrite this sentence: *She stepped in, and he turned to follow her.*

## BODY MOVEMENTS

Many authors waste WC by including reports of trivial body movements. Here's an example: *Maggie cocked her head, trying to place the man.*

It's not necessary to tell us what Maggie did with her head as she tried to place the man. Cutting *cocked her head* wouldn't affect the plot in the slightest, plus it cuts three WC. A rewrite looks like this: *Maggie tried to place the man.*

Here's another example of excessive details about body movements: *Arching her back, she stood and walked to the window.* This 10-word sentence can be reduced to 5:

BEFORE: *Arching her back, she stood and walked to the window.*
AFTER: *She walked to the window.*
BEFORE WC: 10
AFTER WC: 5
GAINED WC: 5

Details about insignificant body movements, such as those in the sentence above add nothing of value to drabbles. It doesn't matter that she arched her back. Nor is it necessary to tell us she stood before walking to the window. These details work best in novels and short stories, but never in drabbles.

If the sentence about arching her back is unnecessary, so are all other minute body movements, including blinking, turning toward, stooping, clenching teeth, raising eyebrows, and so forth.

Let's look at more examples and how sentences can be rewritten to remove trivial details about body movements:

BEFORE: *Barry clenched his fist and knocked.*
AFTER: *Barry knocked.*

BEFORE WC: 6
AFTER WC: 2
GAINED WC: 4

BEFORE: *Ed reached over and with this left hand turned off the radio.*
AFTER: *Ed turned off the radio.*
BEFORE WC: 12
AFTER WC: 5
GAINED WC: 7

Q15: Rework this sentence: *Mikey gulped and took a step back, but the man's words held his attention.*

Q16: Fix this one: *Tucking her long, dark hair behind her ears, she ate lunch.*

Q17: Change this to meet minimalist objectives: *Sam's jaw dropped, and he started to protest.*

Q18: Rewrite this sentence to eliminate trivial body movements: *A woman entered the kitchen through the back door, wiping her hands on her garden apron.*

Q19: Reduce WC in this sentence: *Molly ran shrieking, her pigtails flying, trying to get away from the other kids in the game of hide and seek.*

Q20: See what you can do with this one: *She beamed, stretched, yawned nervously, and said, "I love you, too!"*

Other kinds of trivial body movements, such as sighs, smiles, nods, head shakes, and shrugs appear so often in drabbles, that we discuss them in detail below.

## SIGHS

We've seen hundreds of reports of characters sighing in drabble narratives. We've also seen dozens of situations in which characters sighed their dialogue instead of saying it, an error involving a said bookism, a subject discussed in the next chapter.

No matter where they show up in drabbles, reports of sighs are nothing more than word-wasting fillers. For example: *Joe sighed when he rubbed his sore ankle.* Whether a character sighed or not while doing something is not significant to the plot of any drabble. It's enough to tell readers: *Joe rubbed his sore ankle.* Removing the sigh in this example saves three WC.

One story had this as an opening sentence: *Sigh!*

Here are some examples of superfluous sighing we've seen in drabbles:

- *Sighing, Mary decided not to answer her husband's nasty remark.*
- *"My little wife," he sighed, brushing fat teardrops from her cheeks,*
- *Carol sighed when she realized another chore had been added to her list.*
- *She sighs. "Yeah."*
- *She sighed dramatically and went back to pour tea in the mugs that her mother had bought at the market in Shanghai.*
- *She took a deep breath and sighed.*
- *Bud sighed. "I know."*
- *He sighs and glances over to his Watch Sergeant.*
- *Mary sighed with relief.*
- *He looked down at the floor and sighed.*
- *She stopped and sighed.*
- *"Let's get this over with," I sighed.*

Q21: How many words can you cut from this sentence? *She took a deep breath and sighed.*

Q22. How many words can you remove from this sentence? *He sighs and glances over to his Watch Sergeant.*

## SMILES

We've seen hundreds of instances where characters smiled in drabbles. Many seemed to occur for no reason. We've also seen dozens of situations in which characters smiled their dialogue instead of saying it, an error involving a said bookism, a subject discussed in the next chapter.

No matter where they show up in drabbles, reports of smiles are nothing more than word-wasting fillers. For example: *Smiling, she crumpled up the paper and tossed it on the ground.*

A character smiling before or after doing or saying something is not significant to the plot of any drabble. It's enough to tell readers: S*he crumpled up the paper and tossed it on the ground.* Cutting the smile in this example saves one WC.

In contrast, we don't recall seeing any reports of characters frowning. Yet, many of the stories gave plenty of reasons to make characters frown. We suggest authors omit reports of frowning as they too serve little or no purpose in 100-word stories.

More examples of characters smiling in drabbles:

BEFORE: *I put on my broadest smile and stepped forward to greet the startled young woman.*
AFTER: *I greeted the startled young woman.*
BEFORE WC: 15
AFTER WC: 6
GAINED WC: 9

Our version cuts nine WC. Besides cutting the smile, we removed the words describing the trivial body movement: *and stepped forward.*

BEFORE: *"Yes, yes, that's right," said the man, smiling again.*
AFTER: *"Yes, that's right," said the man.*
BEFORE WC: 9
AFTER WC: 6
GAINED WC: 3

In this one, we also cut one of the *yes* words, because there's no need to repeat dialogue in drabbles. Repeating words in dialogue wastes words and doesn't add anything of value to the story. Our version cuts three WC.

Q23: Fix this sentence: *Carol smiled at the driver, and waved to her children.*

Q24: Rewrite this sentence: *Smiling weakly, she greeted Linda with a soft, "Hello."*

Q25: Make this conform to minimalist objectives: *She came to the door, and I smiled, "Hello, my love."*

Q26: Reduce WC: St*ill smiling, Sandy rested against the back of the couch.*

Q27: Rework this sentence: *Sophia turned off the computer and smiled to herself.*

Here are two more examples:

BEFORE: *"Oh." He smiled again. The taller guy flashed me this huge smile.*
AFTER: *"Oh," he said.*
BEFORE WC: 12
AFTER WC: 3
GAINED WC: 9

Notice how the BEFORE version gave two different smiling characters. By dropping the second sentence and rewriting the first sentence, we cut nine WC count, which is almost 10% of a drabble's total.

BEFORE: *The aisle was empty and Sandra smiled.*
AFTER: *The aisle was empty.*
BEFORE WC: 7
AFTER WC: 4
GAINED WC: 3

The examples below cannot be repaired. They should've been deleted from manuscripts:

- *She smiled back in familiar longing.*
- *He smiled and cocked one eyebrow.*
- *Lisa smiled. Joe smiled back.*
- *I smiled at her again, the puzzlement mine this time.*
- *He gave her a half smile.*
- *Something-or-other smiled sweetly, and left.*
- *I smiled and she smiled back.*
- *I managed a faint smile.*
- *He turned to Susan and smiled.*

**NODS**

Example: *Nodding affirmatively, Jim said, "Yes."*

More examples:

- *All she did was nod politely.*
- *"Every day," I nodded my head.*
- *The old man nodded before he spoke.*
- *Cynthia returned the nod.*
- *The man returned the nod.*
- *The waitress pursed her lips but merely nodded.*

- *The boy studied the kelp and nodded.*
- *Ethan nods and grunts at the appropriate junctures.*

Notice that in some sentences a character returned a nod. This means the author had to tell us one character nodded first, then a second character returned the nod. Imagine how much WC could be gained if the whole idea of nodding were omitted.

Here's the final example:

*"Are you okay?" he asked.*
*She ran her fingers over the carvings on the table and nodded her head.*

Note how the second sentence uses 14 words to tell us what she did with her fingers before nodding. It also includes a needless detail by explaining what body part she used to nod.

Here's a situation in which the second sentence could be reduced considerably by replacing the narrative with dialogue, as shown below:

BEFORE: *She ran her fingers over the carvings on the table and nodded her head.*
AFTER: *"Yes."*
BEFORE WC: 14
AFTER WC: 1
GAINED WC: 13

Remember: when characters are nodding, nothing dynamic or important is happening.

**HEAD SHAKES**

We've seen dozens of instances in which characters shook their heads before doing something. Here's an example: *Charlie shook his head, then spoke.*

This is useless filler that does nothing for the plot. If the report about Charlie shaking his head had been left out, it wouldn't have diminished the impact of the plot in the slightest.

Four WC is saved by cutting: *shook his head, then,* as shown below:

BEFORE: *Charlie shook his head, then spoke.*
AFTER: *Charlie spoke.*
BEFORE WC: 6
AFTER WC: 2
GAINED WC: 4

When tempted to add this kind of filler to your stories, ask yourself: which is more important to the story—the fact that Charlie shook his head, or the fact that Charlie spoke?

Q28: Fix this sentence: *The old woman shook her head as she continued to peel potatoes.*

Q29: Rewrite this one: *Lisa shook her head, then spoke*

**SHRUGS**

We've noticed many instances in which a character shrugs before giving an answer to a question. This serves no useful purpose in drabbles. Here's an example: *Terry shrugged then said, "I guess I'll have some ice cream."* Cutting *shrugged then* cuts two WC.

More examples:

- *"Oh well, I'll try again next week," Harriet shrugged.*
- *She shrugged and told him to drink up.*

Note that in the first sentence, Harriet didn't speak the words, she shrugged them. Nobody can shrug words; thus, this is an example of a said bookism, a subject covered in the next chapter.

## COOKBOOK PROCEDURES

This occurs when authors detail each step a character does to perform a task. Usually it involves a mundane activity that needs no explanation.

Here's an example: *She stood up, went to the window, raised the shade, opened the window, and looked outside.*

This is easily fixed by rewriting: *She went to the window and looked outside.* Whether or not she had to stand, raise the shade, and open the window before looking outside are superfluous to the plot when an author has only 100 words to create a complete story.

Another example: *He reached out, grasped the door handle, pressed on it, then pulled on the door to get inside the car.*

Q30: How would you fix this sentence? *He reached out, grasped the door handle, pressed on it, then pulled on the door to get inside the car.*

Another error some writers make when including cookbook-style procedures is when they tell us where body parts are situated at any given time. Here's an example: *Stomping across the kitchen, Sally stood in front of her mother with her hands planted on each hip, and said...* This sentence wastes words telling us where Sally's hands were, as well as her geographical position in relation to her mother.

The fact that Sally stomped across the kitchen and stood in front of her mother, plus the location of her hands might work well as a visual for a novel or short story. However those details are superfluous for drabbles. Here's how we'd rewrite the sentence:

BEFORE: *Stomping across the kitchen, Sally stood in front of her mother with her hands planted on each hip, and said...*
AFTER: *Sanding before her mother, Sally said...*
BEFORE WC: 20
AFTER WC: 6
GAINED WC: 14

Remember that you aren't writing a novel. Use word economy at all times. It's not necessary to explain to readers every step a character must perform to complete an act.

## IMPOSSIBLE MANNERISMS

Authors sometimes describe a character's mannerisms that seem impossible to perform. Here are some examples:

- *The old man nodded sagely.*

- *He ends the night none the wiser, just a shriveled dusty thing with an almost-smile.*
- *He glanced one more time at the apartment complex and swallowed his breath.*
- *A heavy man walks past with one eye forward and circles back.*
- *With an almost visible shrug, she turned and walked back towards the way she came.*

Based on the five examples above, we have to ask how somebody nods sagely, how does somebody give an almost-smile, how does a character swallow his breath, how does a man walk past with one eye forward, and what is an almost visible shrug?

We always cite sentences like this in our critiques by saying, "If you can't look in a mirror and repeat mannerisms you attribute to your characters, don't include those mannerisms in your stories."

Consider this one: *Laura spoke just above a whisper.*

We wonder how somebody speaks just above a whisper. At what point does a whisper end and more audible speech begin? If you can't answer this question and demonstrate what it means to speak just above a whisper, don't include statements like this in your drabbles. Put the WC to better use by making your plot more compelling.

More examples:

- *They stared at Caron with those undeniable looks.*
- *The captain's gray eyes challenged the skies as they began to turn black.*
- *Her gaze pierced the glass door and falling snow.*
- *Her boss looked at her with vague curiosity.*

- *Grimly, she waved her hand in the direction of the star cluster.*
- *Eyes burning with humiliation, Marty barely noticed men in black dusters entering when he left.*

After reading the above, we wondered how somebody stared with undeniable looks, how eyes challenged the skies, and how a gaze pierced falling snow. We wondered what pierced, falling snow looked like. We wondered how a character looked at somebody with vague curiosity. We wondered how anyone waves a hand grimly. Finally, we wondered how somebody's eyes burn when they feel humiliation.

Some of the sentences shown above can be saved. Let's look at these examples:

BEFORE: *Grimly, she waved her hand in the direction of the star cluster.*
AFTER*: She waved in the direction of the star cluster.*
BEFORE WC: 12
AFTER WC: 9
GAINED WC: 3

BEFORE: *The captain's gray eyes challenged the skies as they began to turn black.*
AFTER: *The captain's gray eyes turned black.*
BEFORE WC: 13
AFTER WC: 6
GAINED WC: 7

Q31: See if you can save this sentence: *He glanced one more time at the apartment complex and swallowed his breath.*

Q32: Rewrite this one: *Looking at the disheveled man, Charlie swallowed down his disgust.*

Q33: Fix the sentence: *Eyes burning with humiliation, Marty barely noticed men in black dusters entering when he left.*

Here are more examples of impossible mannerisms:

- *She answered him with a tight smile.*
- *He leaned forward anxiously.*
- *Harry glanced up and offered a clueless smile.*
- *Standing behind the counter, she gave him this root beer float kind of smile*

Always avoid ascribing to your characters mannerisms that people can't possibly perform. Omitting them always saves WC.

**PAUSES**

Pauses occur when authors have their characters slow down or stop all activities in a scene. This should be omitted from drabbles, because stories are supposed to move forward quickly. Needless pauses always waste WC and stall the story.

Here's a list of pauses we've encountered in drabbles.

- *After a long pause he said no.*
- *I hesitated, but only for a moment.*
- *She paused, then checked the box marked middle bedroom, exterior.*

- *Ed slowly turned toward her.*
- *He hesitated, drinking his apple juice.*
- *He paused, then stepped into the trees.*
- *There was some silence before he spoke.*
- *Alex paused and then said...*
- *He paused to consider his options.*
- *He paused long and deliberate, daring anyone to goad him.*
- *Joe and I stared at each other, motionless.*
- *He stared hard at the crumpled packet for a few seconds.*
- *He said two words, shook his head, and paused a long time before continuing.*

Looking at the last example, we wonder what a drabble gains by including a long pause in which a character accomplishes nothing. We also wonder why the character had to shake his head, a trivial action that also accomplishes nothing in a drabble.

Most pauses we've seen can't be fixed. They should never have been included. They only burn up WC that could've been put to better use.

Notice how long the unnecessary pause is in this example: *Tucking her long, dark hair behind her ears, she took a deep breath and held it. Exhaled. Took another one, held it longer, and then finally answered him.*

The character should've answered the male character immediately. Not doing so wasted 28 WC without adding anything of value to the plot. At this point, the story was stalled.

Here's another we've seen: *I stood planted, not going anywhere.* We wondered why six words were expended to stall the story.

This needless pause was stuck in the middle of two lines of dialogue: *She paused to fill in a corner of her drawing.*

Here's one that appeared right before a story's final sentence: *Al looked and took a moment to regain his breath before turning the business card over.* The next sentence told us what the card said, so this sentence could have been eliminated without impacting the plot.

In this example, WC was wasted to tell us a character barely paused: *"You leave on another of your 'missions',"* she began *barely pausing for breath, "and you don't come back for over three days!"*

Q34: Though most sentences containing needless pauses can't be fixed, here's one that can. See what you can do with it: *After a pause, I asked, "What does it mean?"*

## ENTRANCES AND EXITS

We've read many drabbles in which too many words were used to get characters into and out of a scene. Here are some examples:

- *I climbed the stairs, knocked on his office door and went inside.*
- *He led me out of the office into the corridor.*
- *He opened a 'Restricted Access' door, looked around it into the following corridor, looked at me and put a finger to his lips. We reached its end and quietly climbed up some unlit stairs and came to a landing.*
- *The door opened and a man in faded jeans and western shirt sauntered in. He stood quiet for a few seconds, then headed toward Kincaid's table.*

Let's look at how we can speed up these entrances and exits...

BEFORE: *I climbed the stairs, knocked on his office door and went inside.*
AFTER: *I knocked on his office door and entered.*
BEFORE WC: 12
AFTER WC: 8
GAINED WC: 4

BEFORE: *He opened a 'Restricted Access' door, looked around it into the following corridor, looked at me and put a finger to his lips. We reached its end and quietly climbed up some unlit stairs and came to a landing.*
AFTER*: We left through a "Restricted Access" door, and came to a landing.*
BEFORE WC: 39
AFTER WC: 12
GAINED WC: 27

Q35: How would you trim WC in this one? *He led me out of the office into the corridor.*

Q36: Fix this one: T*he door opened and a man in faded jeans and western shirt sauntered in. He stood quiet for a few seconds, then headed toward Kincaid's table.*

## FLASHBACKS

Always omit flashbacks, because they move the story backward. Here's an example in which the author opens with a grabber, then suddenly gives us a flashback:

*Susan stepped into the house that was proclaimed the most haunted in world for the year 2020.*

*She remembered other haunted houses she'd examined out of curiosity. That was way back in 1999 when her dad was still alive, and she'd worked for a large electronics firm.*

The story began with the idea that Susan had stepped into the most haunted house in the world for the year 2020. That's quite a grabber for horror fans. We expected to read exciting details of what happened next. However, the author decided not to tell us. Instead she gave us 30 words of history about Susan's past activities beginning in the year 1999. Meanwhile, the story moved backward.

If authors insist on letting us know a bit about a character's past, we suggest they do it in as few words as possible. For example, if a distraught person is about to jump off a bridge, it's okay if a character asks why. The protagonist can give a short answer, and then the story should move forward to its conclusion.

On the other hand, if a writer decides to take readers back to, say, three months ago, and detail how the protagonist was abandoned by the woman he loved, the story has gone backward. It's enough for the jumper to say he lost his girlfriend. Then the story should move forward.

Another way to avoid flashbacks is to start the story at a different place.

Q37: From the minimalist point of view, why should we cut flashbacks from drabbles?

This concludes Chapter 5. The next chapter discusses how to develop minimalist dialogue for drabbles.

## ANSWERS TO QUESTIONS

Q1: Cuts one WC each time.

Q2: When the character is famous, such as George Washington.

Q3: They waste one word each time they appear. However, if you use only last names, then don't include first names for the same reason.

Q4: Might throw readers out of the story as they stop reading to figure out how the name is pronounced.

Q5: *Dr. Harlow taught a Psychology course at the university. Charlie decided to take the course. On the first day of class, he went to the room where Harlow was supposed to teach. Instead of Harlow, he found somebody else sitting at a desk facing the class.*

Q6: Sarah wore black shoes.

Q7: The door opened. A man walked in. By changing one sentence into two sentences, we cut seven WC.

Q8: "I hate you!" Sara said.

Q9: Liz said, "I'm very angry with you!" or "I'm very angry with you," Liz said. Doesn't matter in a drabble how her face looked when she said it. Note that we rewrote the sentence by rearranging the words.

Q10: He raised his pistol. Doesn't matter what his face looked like at the time.

Q11: Joe shaved.

Q12: He threw a rock.

Q13: As he left, the streetlight flickered.

Q14: She stepped in, and he followed.

Q15: The man's words held Mikey's attention.

Q16: She ate lunch.

Q17: Sam protested.

Q18: A women entered the kitchen through the back door.

Q19: Shrieking, Molly ran from the kids playing hide and seek.

Q20: She said, "I love you, too!"

Q21: Two

Q22: Two

Q23: Carol waved to her children.

Q24: She said, "Hello," to Linda. We deleted the word *soft*, because we aren't certain what a *soft hello* sounds like. Also, it doesn't matter exactly how she said the word *hello*. We didn't mention the greeting, because saying "Hello," is a greeting.

Q25: She came to the door, and I said, "Hello, my love."

Q26: Sandy rested against the couch.

Q27: Sophia turned off the computer.

Q28: The old woman peeled potatoes.

Q29: Lisa spoke.

Q30: He got into the car.

Q31: He glanced one more time at the apartment complex.

Q32: Charlie felt disgusted when he saw the disheveled man.

Q33: Marty barely noticed men in black dusters entering when he left.

Q34: I asked, "What does it mean?"

Q35: We left his office.

Q36: Several ways to rewrite this. Here's one: The door opened. A man entered and approached Kincaid's table.

Q37: Flashbacks move the story backward. Drabbles should always move forward.

# CHAPTER 6: DEVELOPING MINIMALIST DIALOGUE

This chapter discusses how to meet minimalist objectives when developing dialogue in your drabbles.

Include the following in dialogue to achieve word economy

- **Concise Dialogue**
- **Contractions**
- **Substandard English**

Omit the following to achieve word economy:

- **Unclear Dialogue**
- **Action Tags**
- **Repetition**
- **Interruptions**
- **Slang**
- **Foreign Words**
- **Regional Dialects**
- **Idiomatic Expressions**
- **Said Bookisms**
- **Speaking Descriptions**

Let's look at the first item to see how it impacts your drabble…

## CONCISE DIALOGUE

Always control your characters' dialogue by making it as concise as possible. One way to do that is to avoid wordy sentences. Here are some examples:

BEFORE: *"Why does my head hurt so gosh darn much?"*
AFTER: *"Why does my head hurt?"*
BEFORE WC: 9
AFTER WC: 5
GAINED WC: 4

BEFORE: *"Where are you gonna go now?"*
AFTER: *"Where are you going?"*
BEFORE WC: 6
AFTER WC: 4
GAINED WC: 2

Q1: Make this dialogue more concise: *"Well if you are not a doctor, what, if I may ask, are you, anyway?"*


Q2: See what you can do to make this more concise. *"I'll look like a wimp hanging out dressed as a vampire,"* said Harry.


## CONTRACTIONS

Convert words to contractions every chance you have when writing dialogue. Each instance cuts one WC.

For example, if you write this sentence: *I am terribly sorry,* you can save one word by changing *I am* to *I'm.* This also makes dialogue smoother and more natural-sounding.

Here are some examples of contractions:

- *I'll* replaces *I will.*
- *It'd* replaces *It would.*

- *You're* replaces *You are.*
- *I'd promised Susan I wouldn't gamble* replaces *I had promised Susan I would not gamble.*

Here are some before and after examples:

BEFORE: *"I am sick."*
AFTER: *"I'm sick."*
BEFORE WC: 3
AFTER WC: 2
GAINED WC: 1

BEFORE: *"She is gonna shoot."*
AFTER: "She's gonna shoot."
BEFORE WC: 4
AFTER WC: 3
GAINED WC: 1

Q3: Rewrite this sentence by using contractions. *"I would like it if he would walk me home, because, frankly, I am scared of the dark.*

Q4: How many contractions did you form when you rewrote the above sentence?

## SUBSTANDARD ENGLISH

Another way to trim words is to use substandard English. You can save one WC each time. Here are some examples:

STANDARD: *"I want to buy a car."*
SUBSTANDARD: *"I wanna buy a car."*

STANDARD: *"I have to run an errand."*
SUBSTANDARD: *"I hafta run an errand."*

STANDARD: *"I got to borrow money."*
SUBSTANDARD: *"I gotta borrow money."*

STANDARD: *"I'm going to get a new job."*
SUBSTANDARD" *"I'm gonna get a new job."*

We've often used this kind of substandard English in our drabbles to save WC. No magazine or contest editor has ever rejected our work for doing so.

Q5: Make this sentence substandard to cut one WC: *"I should have gone home."*

## UNCLEAR DIALOGUE

Always strive to make your characters' dialogue as clear as possible. If you fail to do that, you may end up throwing editors out of the story. It's a sure way to get your submission rejected.

Here's an example of unclear dialogue: *"Come and go,"* I *pleaded with Charlie.*

On one hand the speaker is asking somebody to come with him, and in the same sentence wants the person to do the opposite.

This example has two lines of unclear dialogue:

*"And that's a sala-war?"*

*"Salwaar Kameez."*

When we encountered the above dialogue, we were tossed out of the story.

## ACTION TAGS

To understand the function of action tags in a sentence containing dialogue, look at the illustration below, which includes the sentence: *"I'm sorry," she said, wringing her hands and sighing.*

| Dialogue | Dialogue Tag | Action Tag |
|----------|--------------|------------|
| I'm sorry | she said | wringing her hands and sighing |

Action tags account for the largest amount of wasted WC we find in drabbles. Authors use them to describe every possible kind of bodily movement, no matter how insignificant, such as:

- Blinking
- Leaning
- Nodding
- Raising
- Rolling
- Scratching
- Shifting
- Shrugging
- Sighing
- Sniffing
- Turning
- Twisting

Novels and short stories are often loaded with action tags, because creative writing courses and how-to books tell us they can help define characters. Since genre drabbles are too short to focus on character-development, you should strive to omit superfluous action tags. Here's why:

- They burn up WC needlessly.
- They can be distracting, because they often intrude and draw attention to themselves.
- They often contain trivial details.
- They usually don't add anything of value to the plot.
- They add a reader expectation that the tag reveals something and the reader is disappointed when this expectation is not met

Q6: Name at least two reasons we gave you for omitting trivial action tags in drabble dialogue.

When we encounter drabbles with trivial action tags—and some include them after every line of dialogue—we suspect immediately the story has little or zero plot.

Here's an illustration of a sentence that contains action tags and what happens when we remove them:

WITH ACTION TAGS                 NO ACTION TAGS

*"Done that." Harley chewed*          *"Done that."*
*his pen, snapping the tip of*
*his teeth*

The drabble in which this appeared was about first contact with aliens from outer space. When we read it, we couldn't fathom why the author wasted 10% of the story's entire WC telling us a guy chewed a pen, and what it did to his teeth, and even what part of his teeth.

More examples of dialogue in which trivial action tags burned up WC unnecessarily in drabbles:

- *"After you," I said, as we followed a well-dressed man and his date through the door.*
- *"Do you think aliens really exist?" I asked, as I scratched my itchy nose.*
- *"It's the farm over there." The deceased's husband dried his hands with a tea towel.*

Q7: List the trivial action tag in this sentence: *"After you," I said, as we followed a well-dressed man and his date through the door.*

Q8: What's the trivial action tag in this sentence: *"Do you think aliens really exist?" I asked, as I scratched my itchy nose.*

Q9: Fix this sentence by removing the trivial action tag: *"Hello," Marie said, making her voice sound deep.*

Trivial action tags can appear in front of dialogue. Here's an example: *She shook her head, "How can that be good?"*

Delete trivial action tags in the sentences below and rewrite them the minimalist way.

Q10: *She leaned forward, as though to draw closer to the caller. "Yes, my name is Helen."*

Q11: *"I thought the price was for a round-tip," the husband said as he gritted his teeth and shook his head.*

Q12: *Scraping his foot against the chair, Bill asked, "Can I have more pie?"*

Q13: *Toback leans in close to me, his shoulders descending from his neck as if a lead weight were hanging on them, sighs without remorse and says: "You take too much."*

Q14: *Scratching her knee, she asked, "Where is the Embassy?"*

Q15: *At this, the wife turned to her husband, "Dear, perhaps we should reconsider."*

Q16: *The NASA boss scrunched his face up, "Come again?"*


Q17: *Turning her face slowly up at me, she whispered, "Thank you..." her eyes fighting opening as if she was awakening under a blinding light.*


Q18: Rewrite this sentence to meet minimalist objectives: *"Do I have to go in today?" Jonathan asked while pulling up his pants and sliding out of bed.*


Q19: Identify the trivial action tags in these two sentences, and rewrite them:

*"I returned the favor," the businessman forced himself to grin. "It wasn't a favor," the salesman replied, twisting his cigarette to death.*


At this point, we've been discussing *trivial* action tags that should be omitted from drabbles.

However, we don't want to give you the impression that all action tags are trivial. Here are two examples in which action tags fit the situation:

- *"Get on the examination table, or you'll be a dead Earthman," yelled the Martian, as he pointed a ray gun at Harry.*
- *Slapping handcuffs across my wrists, she said, "You're under arrest!"*

## REPETITION

Repetition is another word-waster in dialogue. Here's an example: *"He talks all the time. All the time," Tom said.*

Q20: Rewrite Tom's dialogue to conform to minimalist objectives.

Here are more examples:

BEFORE: *"Max picked up an extremely attractive alien in a sushi bar, where he wined her and dined her, then wined her some more."*
AFTER: *"Max picked up an extremely attractive alien in a sushi bar, where he wined and dined her."*
BEFORE WC: 23
AFTER WC: 17
GAINED WC: 6

BEFORE: *"Ten dollars!" he'd say. "They only want ten dollars! Ten dollars and you can have whatever you want."*
AFTER: *"Ten dollars and you can have whatever you want," he'd say.*
BEFORE WC: 18
AFTER WC: 11
GAINED WC: 7

BEFORE: *"No, no, no. That's my great uncle."*
AFTER: *"No, that's my great uncle."*

BEFORE WC: 7
AFTER WC: 5
GAINED WC: 2

BEFORE: *"Die. Die. Die,"* she yelled, *trying to kill the giant squid.*
AFTER: *"Die,"* she yelled, *trying to kill the giant squid.*
BEFORE WC: 11
AFTER WC: 9
GAINED WC: 2

BEFORE: *"Well, officer, you see, I was…I was trying to kill a fly."*
AFTER: *"Well, officer, I was trying to kill a fly."*
BEFORE WC: 13
AFTER WC: 9
GAINED WC: 4

Note: When using the word count facility of Microsoft WORD for the BEFORE sentence, we got a WC of 12. That's incorrect, and was caused by the appearance of the three dots. Counting the words by hand, we came up with 13. Remember this potential for WC errors, when your final draft contains three dots (ellipsis) between two words.

Q21: Rewrite this example: *"Harry, I'm beginning to believe in zombies. I'm beginning to believe it."*

Q22: How would you remove repetition from this sentence? *"Give me a beer,"* said the stranger. *"A draft beer."*

## INTERRUPTIONS

We've seen lots of examples where one character's dialogue is interrupted by another. When that happens, we never discover what the character wanted to say.

Here's an example:  *One of them said,  "The hours are a good—"*

In another example, we discovered the character's dialogue was interrupted by the author so trivial details could be included about head shaking and pausing: *"Trains, though—" He shook his head and paused a long time before continuing. "Ain't been no trains for years."*

Q23: How would you rewrite the sentences directly above? HINT: Combine everything into one sentence. Don't forget to indicate who is speaking.

Here's another example: *"I'm as real as —" I broke off, realizing the stupidity of what I'd started to say.*

Since the character thought his own dialogue was stupid, we wondered why the author wasted 16 WC writing this sentence.

Note: When using the word count facility of Microsoft WORD for the sentence above, we got a WC of 17. That's incorrect, and was caused by the appearance of the dash. Counting the words by hand, we came up with 16. Remember this potential for WC errors, when your final draft contains a dash after a word.

Another kind of interruption we've seen in drabbles is when two characters are exchanging dialogue, and the author interrupts the dialogue with a sentence containing trivial narrative. Here's an example:

*"I'm going to slit your throat," Lisa shouted.*
*The wind lightly blew her dark brown hair into Jim's face before he could answer.*
*"Do that, and you'll never find out where I hid the money," said Jim.*

The sentence that interrupts the dialogue contains 15 words of trivial details. That amounts to 15% of the drabble's total WC.

## SLANG

Slang can date your story, making it obsolete. Today's popular slang may disappear tomorrow. It may also be unclear to those who are not familiar with the expression. Slang can also throw editors out of the story as they pause to figure out what the words mean. Further, some slang uses more words than it replaces. Here are some examples:

- *up for grabs = available*
- *drunk as a skunk = very intoxicated*
- *done in = tired*
- *baloney = nonsense*
- *bananas = hysterical or crazy*
- *dingbat = idiot*
- *steamed up = angry*
- *take a hike = leave*
- *break it up = stop*
- *catch some Z's = sleep*

## FOREIGN WORDS

Don't include foreign words. Example: *"Miren, miren, las liebritas!"* Many editors might not know what this means, and may be thrown out of the story.

The appearance of foreign words can give the impression that authors are trying to convey a high level of sophistication. Here are some examples of dozens we've seen in drabbles:

- *au courant*
- *bonne chance*
- *carte blanche*
- *c'est la vie*
- *vol-au-vents*
- *ad hoc*
- *de facto*
- *quid pro quo*
- *"Si! Mucha experiencia."*

Here's an example in which three Latin words appeared as the final sentence of a drabble: *Audaces fortuna iuvat.* This greatly diminished what had been an interesting fantasy tale. It was the first time we'd ever been thrown out of a story when reading a story's last sentence.

We were thrown out of a drabble when encountering this sentence: *"You are a queso grande*,"* Chico told Parmesano.* The asterisk in the first sentence aroused our curiosity, until we found a legend at the end of the drabble that said: * *Big Cheese.* Each asterisk that appeared here counted as one word. The words in the legend used two WC. This way of writing burned up four WC that could have been put to better use in the story.

Here's an example of a story that included an alien who tried his best to speak English: *"Yeh-sihrrr. Me werry hahndy."*

Another example of alien-speak from a drabble: *"Wantneed touchyestouch you with mind stuff."*

All of the above drew attention to themselves, which made us pause and wonder what we were reading. When we did that, we were thrown out of the stories.

We also saw this sentence in a story: *I drew my dagger and gladius.* This threw us out of the story, because we never heard of a gladius.

Remember: don't risk throwing magazine and contest editors out of your story by including foreign words.

## REGIONAL DIALECTS

Some authors think it's necessary to reproduce exactly how various ethnic groups and characters from various parts of the nation speak English. Not only does it slow the read, as we try to pronounce and decipher what's being said, but it can also throw us out of the story. Regional dialect tends to draw attention to itself and away from the story

Here are a few we've seen in stories.

- *"Yer pullin' me leg."*
- *"Tree little boids sittin' on a coib."*
- *"How kin Ah take keer of ol' Bubba without mah thayngs?"*

Notice how you have to reduce your normal reading speed when you encounter dialogue like this.

Although this example is not one of regional dialect, it's an example of an author trying to represent the speech of a drunk: *"'S'NOT MY FAULT. SH'YOURS. SHORE IS."* To make the read even more difficult, the author used upper case characters for every word in the dialogue.

Be sure to omit regional dialects from your drabbles. If you don't, you may irritate editors, as they try to decipher what characters are saying. Editors expect stories that can be read as quickly as possible. Regional dialects in stories always work against that expectation.

## IDIOMATIC EXPRESSIONS

Don't include idiomatic expressions whenever possible. They may be unfamiliar to those whose second language is English.

Many English idiomatic expressions burn up too much WC. Here are some examples:

- *take no account of = don't consider*
- *raise your hand against = hit*
- *drive to distraction = confuse*
- *will be the death of = end*

## SAID BOOKISMS

These show up in dialogue tags as replacements for *said* and *asked*. Here's an example: *"You'll never see a flying saucer, because they don't exist," Harry opined.* In this sentence, *Harry opined* is the dialogue tag, and *opined* is the bookism.

Note how the dialogue itself shows it's Harry's opinion. Then the author tells us it was his opinion by adding the bookism *opined.* This amounts to duplication within in the same sentence. The way to avoid this is to use *said.* Readers can determine the speaker's intent by reading the dialogue. There's no need to remind them by adding a bookism to repeat the same idea.

Here's another example: *"It's a beautiful coat, Elizabeth," Suzy enthused.* The dialogue tag in this sentence is *Suzy enthused.* The bookism is *enthused.*

Another example: *"Yeah,"* *Lisa agreed.* Notice how the dialogue itself shows us that Lisa agreed, and then we're told that she agreed. That's needless repetition.

Q24: Identify the dialogue tag in this sentence: *"Land the craft immediately," Captain Gordon ordered.*

Q25: Which word in this sentence is the said bookism? *"We should turn left at the next planet," Harry articulated.*

Look at this one: *"Oh well, I'll try again next week," Harriet shrugged.*

The reason for avoiding said bookisms is to keep readers from stumbling over unusual bookisms, causing them to pause. When they pause even for a moment, they're thrown out of the story.

Another example: *"Shut your mouth!" Jim cut her off.* Not only do we have the bookism *cut her off,* but we also have repetition. The dialogue itself gives us the idea that Jim is cutting somebody's dialogue off. The narrative tells us the same thing.

The same happens in this sentence: *"Stop it!" the humanoid begged.*

Said bookisms also include adverbials, such as *profoundly, sweetly,* and many others.

More examples of said bookisms we've seen in drabble dialogue:

- *"And," Flynn prompted.*
- *"Put down your weapons," the alien hissed chillily.*
- *"Actually, I am standing right here," he disputed.*
- *"I've missed you," Ted dared to admit.*
- *"What's that strange object hovering over your house?" Charlie asked inquisitively.*
- *"If you want to rob a jewelry store, you'll need a foolproof plan," Jesse offered helpfully.*
- *"Let go of me, or I'll blow your brains out," she said threateningly.*
- *"Get the hell out of here," she ordered.*

Here's a partial list of some bookisms that can make editors frown:

- *Rumbled*
- *Badgered*
- *Insisted*
- *Crowed*
- *Chimed in*
- *Enunciated*
- *Laughed*
- *Tut-tutted*
- *Hooted angrily*
- *Blurted out*
- *Sighed*
- *Smiled*
- *Sputtered*
- *Intoned*
- *Barked evasively*
- *Begged*
- *Offered*
- *Grunted icily*
- *Announced*
- *Gushed*
- *Seethed sarcastically*

- *Spat back*
- *Persisted*
- *Demanded*
- *Droned*
- *Trilled*
- *Snorted*

Here are more examples, as they're used in dialogue:

- *"Never had this problem before with an interstellar spacecraft," he growled.*
- *"Tell me a bit about yourself," she directed.*
- *"You sure look like you need some," I said, affecting a shoddier grammar.*
- *"I know what that strange object is," he said patiently.*
- *"I'm not your friend!" The spirit shrilled.*
- *"Don't," Cassie simply said.*
- *"We don't mix with the others," he spat.*
- *"Woman," I'd breathe.*

Q26: Identify the said bookism in this sentence: *"Go ahead, see if you can hit my nose," he dared.*

Q27: Identify the said bookism in this sentence: *"This vitamin drink is making me feel like the Emperor of Mars," he crowed zestfully.*

Q28: Based on what you've seen so far, which of the following has the potential for wasting the most WC in a single sentence?

    a.  Foreign words
    b.  Idiomatic expressions
    c.  Slang
    d.  Bookisms

Q29: Name one of the negative effects to your story when you include regional dialogue.

Q30: The word zestfully is an example of an adverbial form of:

    a.  Said bookism
    b.  Needless repetition
    c.  Slang
    d.  Idiomatic expression

Q31: Which is a characteristic of slang?

    a.  It's perfect for drabbles.
    b.  It's always current.
    c.  It makes the read more enjoyable.
    d.  Lots of readers might not understand it.

## SPEAKING DESCRIPTIONS

Don't waste WC describing how a character is speaking. For example: *He hissed his words.*

Here are more examples we've seen in drabbles.

- *She spoke to him with a tinge of sorrow in her voice.*
- *My voice is smoky and low.*
- *She spoke to herself, only slightly audibly.*
- *He spoke more forcefully now, apparently warming to the role.*
- *I speak candidly.*
- *He spoke coldly.*
- *He replied calmer than she expected.*
- *His voice sounded parched and gravelly.*
- *She replied with a sense of confidence.*
- *Boris put on an immaculate Midwest accent.*

None of the above were vital to the plots of the drabbles in which they appeared. In every instance, they merely wasted WC that could've been put to better use by creating more compelling plots.

In most cases, descriptions of how characters speak can't be rewritten. It's best not to include them. Readers want to know what characters say in drabbles, not how they say it.

This concludes Chapter 6. The next chapter discusses how to develop minimalist narrative.

**ANSWERS TO QUESTIONS**

Q1: "If you're not a doctor, what are you?"
Q2: "I'll look wimpy dressed as a vampire," said Harry.
Q3: I'd like it if he'd walk me home, because I'm scared of the dark.
Q4: We formed three.
Q5: "I shoulda gone home."
Q6: Any two of the following:
- They burn up WC needlessly.

- They can be distracting, because they often intrude and draw attention to themselves.
- They often contain trivial details.
- They don't add anything of value to the plot.
- They add a reader expectation that the tag reveals something and the reader is disappointed when this expectation is not met

Q7: As we followed a well-dressed man and his date through the door.

Q8: As I scratched my itchy nose.

Q9: "Hello," Marie said.

Q10: "Yes, my name is Helen."

Q11: "I thought the price was for a round-trip," the husband said.

Q12: Bill asked, "Can have more pie?"

Q13: Toback says, "You take too much."

Q14: "Where is the Embassy?" she asked.

Q15: The wife said to her husband, "Dear, perhaps we should reconsider." We changed *turned* to *said*.

Q16: *"Come again?"* asked the NASA boss.

Q17: She whispered, "Thank you."

Q18: "Do I have to go in today?" Jonathan asked.

Q19: "I returned the favor," the businessman said.
"It wasn't a favor," said the salesman.

Q20: "He talks all the time," Tom said.

Q21: "Harry, I'm beginning to believe in zombies."

Q22: "Give me a draft beer," said the stranger. Or: The stranger said, "Give me a draft beer."

Q23: "Ain't been no trains for years," he said.

Q24: Captain Gordon ordered.

Q25: Articulated.

Q26: Dared

Q27: The adverbial form: crowed zestfully.

Q28: b. Idiomatic expressions

Q29: Either of these two:

- Slows the read, as readers try to pronounce and decipher what's being said.

- Can throw readers out of the story.

Q30: a. Said bookism

Q31: d. Lots of readers might not understand it. Because of that, they might be thrown out of the story as they pause to consider what the slang means.

# CHAPTER 7: DEVELOPING MINIMALIST NARRATIVE - PART 1

This chapter discusses how to meet minimalist objectives for narrative in your drabbles.

The following should be omitted to achieve word economy.

- **Inflated Prose**
- **Trivial Details**
- **Ornate Prose**
- **Similes**
- **Repetition**
- **Facts Of Existence**
- **What Isn't**
- **"And"**
- **"The and That"**

The following should be converted to achieve word economy:

- **Numbers**

Let's look at the first item to see how it can negatively impact your drabble…

**INFLATED PROSE**

Inflated prose occurs in narrative when authors use too many words to describe something. Here's an example: *The boy slumped off down the hall and into his room.*

Too many words were used to tell a simple fact: *The boy went to his room.*

Another example: *Suddenly, a signal flare of an idea lit his mind.* All this means is: *Suddenly, he got an idea.*

Look at this example:

BEFORE: *My brother looked in the direction of my pointed and trembling finger.*
AFTER: *My brother looked where I pointed.*
BEFORE WC: 12
AFTER WC: 6
GAINED WC: 6

Another example: *It refused to go away, even as she screamed at her reflection daily, tearing at the scar until fresh crimson droplets stained the white porcelain sink.*

When we read the drabble in which this sentence appeared, we soon realized the kind of sink and its color didn't matter, because it wasn't vital to the plot. Also, *fresh crimson droplets* is a fancy way of saying *blood*.

To rewrite this, we'd change *fresh crimson droplets stained the white porcelain sink* to: *blood stained the sink.*

Don't imitate this kind of elaborate writing in your drabbles. Remember to be a storyteller first, and writer second. As a storyteller, you wouldn't say to a friend, "Fresh crimson droplets stained the white porcelain sink." If you wouldn't tell a friend a story using words like this, don't do it to drabble readers.

Here are more examples:

BEFORE: *It was only later, back on the ship as it pulled away and headed for Hilo on the Big Island, she came to him.*
AFTER: *She came to him on the ship when it headed for Hilo.*
BEFORE WC: 24
AFTER WC: 12

GAINED WC: 12

BEFORE: *She extended her legs, rising from the bed with fluid grace to stand by his side.*
AFTER: *She got out of bed and stood next to him.*
BEFORE WC: 16
AFTER WC: 10
GAINED WC: 6

BEFORE*: Moments later Sam's scream split the silence.*
AFTER: *Moments later, Sam screamed.*
BEFORE WC: 7
AFTER WC: 4
GAINED WC: 3

Everybody knows silence is broken when somebody screams. Reminding editors of that fact is a waste of words.

BEFORE: *The elusive Chico had clearly striven to cover his tracks, but on the troop's fifth day out, the scout knelt on the dusty plain and pointed to telltale depressions in the dirt.*
AFTER: *Chico covered his tracks, but on the fifth day a scout found them.*
BEFORE WC: 32
AFTER WC: 13
GAINED WC: 19

The BEFORE sentence about Chico contains 32 words, or one third of the entire WC in the drabble. Lots of words were used to tell very little story. Our rewrite used only 13 words to get the idea across.

Using so much WC for a single sentence indicates the more attention was given to writing style than word economy.

BEFORE: *He was making eye contact with all the TV's scattered around the bar.*
AFTER: *He looked at all the TV's scattered around the bar.*
BEFORE WC: 13
AFTER WC: 10
GAINED WC: 3

In the sentence above, *was making eye contact with* is an inflated way of saying *looked at.*

BEFORE: *He read them a story before getting them tucked in for the night.*
AFTER: *He read them a story before bedtime.*
BEFORE WC: 13
AFTER WC: 7
GAINED WC: 6

Notice how *getting them tucked in for the night* is a round-about way of saying *bedtime.*

BEFORE: *Those first waking moments were pain filled, as a hunger surged through my body.*
AFTER: *I woke up feeling hungry.*
BEFORE WC: 14
AFTER WC: 5
GAINED WC: 9

Rewrite the sentences below to make them conform to minimalist objectives.

Q1: *Looking out the dirty window pane, he hazarded a glance at the straw scarecrow.*

Q2: *The words tumbled out of her trembling lips.*

Q3: *Jake's heater shuts down, and, as always, it gurgles a grimy growl, like a dog, a badger, and a death metal singer harmonizing.*

Q4: *Though in point of fact, Uke played the banjo ukulele.*

Q5: *Bob Reece shuffled towards the surgery door, dragging his slightly deadened left leg on the paisley carpet behind him.*

Q6: *The customer browsing in the dried manticore and dragon section of Pete's Priceless Potions, looked up briefly, then made his way out of the front door.*

Q7: *In that hairsbreadth of time before the car skidded out of control, James realized alcohol had blunted his reactions.*

Q8: *She sat at the tiny white cafe table taking fast little breaths as she scribbled on the pad in front of her.*

Q9: *She stood behind the counter, giving him this root-beer float kind of smile.*

Q10: *When my cool friend Chris came strolling along, with the grace and smooth moves of Vanilla Ice on ice (the drug or the frozen water whatever sounds better).*

Q11: *The words she had been waiting for stared back at her in clear bold type.*

Q12: *The twilight-tide sunshine, orange and indigo velvet lit up the endless expanse of highway.*

Q13: *They had gone for a short trip that had now become a nightmare.*

## TRIVIAL DETAILS

Any detail in the story that's not vital to the plot is trivial.

Here's an example: *Sitting at his desk, the NASA boss looked up sharply, as Perkins rushed into his office, all of a dither, and brandishing a piece of paper.*

The trivial details are:

- *Sitting at his desk.* Didn't matter to the story exactly where the boss was positioned.
- *looked up sharply.* What he did with his eyes, and how he did it were superfluous.

Together, these trivial details used seven WC. But there's even more to fix in this sentence, as shown below.

- *Rushed into his office.* This can be changed to: *rushed inside*, cutting two more WC. We can assume the boss was in the office, because he was sitting at his desk.
- *All a dither.* This means *excited.* If we substituted that word, we cut two more WC for a grand total of 11.

When we rewrote the sentence, we examined the meaning carefully, and ended up deleting 14 WC, instead of 11. The new sentence minus trivial details, inflated prose, and unnecessary words looked like this: *Perkins rushed inside the NASA boss's office holding a piece of paper.* This sentence means the same thing as the 26-word one that used more than 25% of the drabble's entire WC.

We also removed *excited,* because Perkins rushed into the office. To us, this implied he was excited about something.

Another example: *Among the white, peppered with black and red lava stones, was the shell.*

We thought the author could've saved ten WC by telling us the character found a shell. The rest was superfluous.

Another example: *The sand felt good, fine as dust in the surging surf.*

After reading the drabble in which this sentence appeared, we decided that the entire 11-word sentence could've been cut. Even if it were necessary to tell us how the protagonist reacted to walking barefoot in the sand, the descriptive words *fine as dust* could've been eliminated. It would've been enough to tell us the sand felt good under the character's feet, which would've shaved five WC.

Delete trivial details in the sentences below. Rewrite them using as few words as possible.

Q14: *Highway fifty divided the land ahead, sage and rocks and sand and salt flats on either side.*

Q15: *Fifty-seven miles to Tampa the green reflective sign read.*

Q16: *He exhaled a puff of smoke in ancestral wonder, primal in reciprocating waves of fog.*

Q17: *The sunshine sowed moted rays of warmth into his bones.*

Trivial details describing how character move their bodies or body parts abound not only in dialogue action tags, but also in narrative. They're usually associated with mundane activities and tend to be nothing more than needless fillers.

Fix these sentences to conform with minimalist objectives:

Q18: *Waiting for her change, the woman adjusted the belt that hugged her slim waist and brushed back her long hair with slight, well-manicured fingers.*

Q19: *I swing my feet up out of the way and lay back so he can sit down on the cot in front of the blue screen and get to it.*

Trivial details often show up in narrative to describe the environment. Here's an example: *Lunar Base IV was shrouded in an artificial darkness which shielded it from curious eyes.*

The trivial detail is: *which shielded it from curious eyes.* If the place was shrouded in darkness, nobody could see it. However, not only was it shielded from curious eyes, but also from eyes that weren't curious. Nobody could see it under any circumstances. Removing this trivial detail cuts six WC.

Another example: *The cell door closed with metallic finality.*

All we need to know is the cell door closed. Describing how it closed is superfluous. Also, *metallic finality* is ambiguous.

Here are some sentences that need to be rewritten the minimalist way:

Q20: *The man pushed some buttons and stared at the screen, brows furrowed.*

Q21: *Each day at five to twelve, the elderly widower, who lived in the small dilapidated cottage at the far end of the village, would walk slowly down to the center of the little hamlet, and stand at the pedestrian crossing expectantly.*

Q22: *After standing there for a few minutes, the old man would turn around and slowly make his way home again, shoulders hunched.*

Q23: *I was drinking a coffee on a terrace when I suddenly heard a terrible barking.*

Q24: *Leaning back against the couch, Sabra thought about the evening.*

## ORNATE PROSE

Don't include ornate prose in genre or anecdotal drabbles. It's often poetic, and loaded with trivial details.

Here's an example of ornate prose: *Crows scatter as she plummets past, riding the ridges and dips, scribing a stuttering line down the mantle of virgin snow.*

The next example uses 40 words, or 40% of the entire drabble: *He ate breakfast on the porch then dragged his wife through the town, pointing out colors bisected by shadow on buildings, birds winging overhead, buttercups licking their chins, fresh lettuce snapping in their mouths, their hands on each other's skin.*

Q25: How would you rewrite the sentence above to cut WC and retain the general idea?

Q26: Rewrite this sentence: *His wife saw the setting sun reflected in a tear on his cheek.*

## SIMILES

Don't waste time and WC devising similes and including them in your drabbles. Here's why:

- Many don't achieve the effect the author intended.
- They draw attention to themselves, especially when they don't work.

- When they're poorly conceived, they can throw editors out of the story.
- They waste WC.
- It isn't necessary to amplify something that was said by adding a simile. For example, it's enough to tell us a character is angry. Editors understand what that means. There's no need to waste words saying she's as mad as a hornet whose nest was just wacked with a broom stick.
- Sometimes we get the impression authors aren't confident in their ability to say something that's mundane, clearly enough. Seems they add a simile to ensure we know for certain what they mean. As noted above, it isn't necessary to further clarify what it means for somebody to be angry. The simile attempts to tell the degree to which the character was angry by comparing it with a hornet's anger. In drabbles that's overkill.

Here's an example of a simile we read in a drabble: *Her knife shone like a distant star in the tropical night.* We thought it was enough to tell us the knife shone.

We weren't sure what the author was driving at in this example: *Brains snag on the fabric of time like hang nails.* Consequently, this threw us out of the story as we tried to decipher this cryptic sentence and cryptic simile.

Here's one that included two similes to make sure readers had absorbed the simple idea of a tree splitting down the middle when struck by lightning: *Lightning hits a tree, splits that tree right down the middle, like a knife slicing an apple, like a saw cutting open a chest.*

Here are more similes that didn't work for us.

- *Without a sound or glance she leaves my bed like a cat in the dark.*
- *Stiff bodies hang like bananas from flora.*

- *He was as blind as a bat in the dark without his glasses and the scent of blood clung to him like a sadistic spice.*
- *She waved his sarcasm away like a summer blue-bottle.*
- *Like a tornado, the three twisted, spun and somersaulted over to the blanket.*
- *I jumped, and the nuts I was measuring spilled and clattered across the kitchen counter like a pyroclastic pecan flow.*
- *I looked at my face in the smashed glass: misshapen but clear, like a moon atop waves.*
- *I sashay across the room, legs and hips and gluteal muscles working together like a NASCAR pit crew.*
- *She sat straight as a breadstick.*
- *The butcher stroked the handle of his chopping knife and winced at her like a driver in his wing mirror after a bump.*
- *The box of dark chocolate mixed creams and nuts beckoned from the coffee table like a beacon in the night, guiding the weary sojourner through choppy waters.*
- *She smells like Venezuela, like rainforest trees when it's raining.*
- *The words crawl out of their mouths like tarantula legs.*
- *This sense of grief, like a smell, hovers over him.*
- *He reached out with the tips of his fingers bunched together by tape and bandage like a semi-naked sock puppet.*
- *Her corpse swung in the wind like a rusty gate.*
- *Civilization calls to her like a Schedule I narcotic.*
- *Brains snag on the fabric of time like hang nails.*

Q27: Remove the simile and rewrite the sentence in as few words as possible: *I sashayed across the room, legs and hips and gluteal muscles working together like a NASCAR pit crew.*

Q28: Fix this sentence to gain WC: *Like a tornado, the three twisted, spun and somersaulted over to the blanket.*

## REPETITION

We're amazed at the number of stories we've read in which authors wasted WC repeating information that was easy to understand. Here's an example: *I heard her. I heard her talking all lovey-dovey to them.*

It's enough to tell us once that the protagonist heard her. It's a simple idea that doesn't have to be repeated.

Another example: *The next evening, she went again. The next evening. And the next.*

We can cut five WC from the above by changing it to: *She went four nights in a row.* That accounts for the first time she went, plus three additional times.

Look at this example: *I read in a magazine recently of a man in America who took one Polaroid each day in his life. Just one.*

Q29: How would you delete words from the sentence above to remove the repetition?

Another example: *It isn't a smell. It's something else— something else.*

We wondered about the logic of these two sentences. If *it* wasn't a smell, logically it had to be something else. Thus, the five words of the second sentence could've been deleted without affecting the plot. Since the author never told us what *it* was, they could've done so by using the five WC gained.

Look at this example: *Wish you were here. Wish you were here.*

This one consists of two fragments: *A hot drink. A sugary hot drink.*

Q30: Fix this sentence: *It really was a miserable party, it really was.*

Here's another: *I blinked. I blinked again. I blinked the final time.*

The second and third sentences should've been deleted to save eight WC.

Q31: Eliminate repetition to cut words: *I miss the lobsters. Yes, I'm from New York and I miss the lobsters.*

Here's one that might throw readers out of the story: *Red, red walls, crimson red, as warm and welcoming as the black-bearded waiter.*

Final Example: *The truth's not worth knowing. It's not.*

Remember that you are always in control of your story's narrative. Ensure you omit repetition in drabbles because it wastes WC. Even worse, it may irritate editors.

## FACTS OF EXISTENCE

Ordinary facts of everyday existence should not be included in a drabble. For example, everyone knows people get wet when they walk without umbrellas on rainy days. Nevertheless, word-wasters like this show up. Here are some examples that we've seen in drabbles:

- *Time marches on.*
- *Grieving is a terrible thing.*
- *Sam's scream split the silence.*
- *Self-control is a slippery thing. You can have it in some ways and not in others.*
- *The human body is so complex.*
- *Some things are better unsaid to avoid problems.*
- *Everything dies sooner or later, that's the truth of it.*

Q32: How would you rewrite this sentence? *Moments later, Sam's scream split the silence.*

## WHAT ISN'T

One of the more unusual waste of words we've seen in drabbles is when authors tell us what characters aren't like, didn't do, didn't feel, didn't think, or almost didn't do.

Here's an example: *She doesn't sit, doesn't turn her back to the fountain.* We're uncertain why the author of this drabble expended 10 words to tell us what a character didn't do. It's one of the many instances in which WC is wasted.

Another example in which words were wasted by telling us something that didn't happen: *His arrival came with no fanfare.* Nothing in the story warranted the mention of the absence of fanfare. Especially since it was about a man entering a store for the first time. The sentence should've been deleted to gain six WC.

Look at this one: *Frustration didn't seem strong enough to describe what she was feeling.* In this case, the author used 11 words, or 11% of the story's WC to tell us how the character didn't feel. We think the character's feelings could've been described in three words: *She was frustrated.*

A few more examples:

- *Detective Lance Cosgrove wasn't a bookworm, but this still seemed just wrong.*
- *I once almost dated a girl.*
- *It wasn't a virus or nuclear war or anything to do with global warming.*
- *He did not look up for a long time.*
- *We wouldn't be knitting tonight, nor planning bake sales, chicken dinners or pancake breakfasts.*
- *He took a sharp breath, and I didn't hear him breathe out.*
- *I drove my horse as fast as she would go, not Servo, that one died in Egypt, but another, a sorrel mare, light and quick as an arrow loosed from the fletcher's grasp in test.*

Let's examine the last example. We wondered why the author named a horse he no longer had, but never named the horse he had. We also pondered why we were told the fate of the horse he no longer had, though the dead horse was not mentioned again for the rest of the story.

Remember to omit statements like this from your story. They serve no purpose except to burn up WC needlessly. Expend WC to tell what characters actually do in a scene.

## "AND"

You can cut one WC each time you remove *and* from a list of items.

BEFORE: *He liked cake, candy and ice cream.*
AFTER: *He liked cake, candy, ice cream.*
BEFORE WC: 7
AFTER WC: 6
GAINED WC: 1

Q33: Rewrite this sentence: *Ronald was tall, dark, handsome, rich, and brilliant.*

## "THE" and "THAT"

You can cut one WC each time you remove an unnecessary *the* or *that* from a sentence. However, when you do make cuts, ensure the result remains a smooth read.

Here is an example:

BEFORE: *Trevor wiped the grease from his lips.*
AFTER: *Trevor wiped grease from his lips.*
BEFORE WC: 7
AFTER WC: 6
GAINED WC: 1

Q34: Fix this sentence: *Harry ate the strange-looking food the aliens gave him.*

Q35: Reduce WC in this sentence: *We stood at the edge of the Martian helium pools.*

Another example:

BEFORE: *The spaceship that landed on the roof had lights that blinked.*
AFTER: *The spaceship that landed on the roof had blinking lights.*
BEFORE WC: 11
AFTER WC: 10
GAINED WC: 1

Q36: Delete unnecessary words: *They all said that she was dead, but he knew that they were lying.*

**NUMBERS**

When using numbers, especially long numbers, substitute digits for words. Example: *She was one hundred and two years old.*

BEFORE: *She was one hundred and two years old.*
AFTER: *She was 102.*
BEFORE WC: 8
AFTER WC: 3
GAINED WC: 5

Q37: Change this sentence: *The gift cost five-seventy-seven with tax.*

This concludes Chapter 7, Part-1. The next chapter discusses more about developing minimalist narrative.

## ANSWERS TO QUESTONS

Q1: Looking out the dirty window, he glanced at the scarecrow.

Q2: Trembling, she spoke.

Q3: Jake's heater shuts down. Doesn't matter in a drabble if it was noisy.

Q4: Uke played the banjo ukulele.

Q5: Bob shuffled toward the surgery door, dragging his left leg behind him.

Q6: The customer browsed the manticor and dragon sections of Pete's Priceless Potions, then left.

Q7: When the car skidded out of control, James realized he was drunk.

Q8: She sat at a café table, scribbling on a pad.

Q9: Several ways to do this. Here's our version: She smiled at him from behind the counter.

Q10: My friend Chris walked by.

Q11: She saw the typewritten words she'd been waiting for.

Q12: Twilight filled the highway.

Q13: Their short trip had become a nightmare.

Q14: Highway 50 divided the land ahead.

Q15: The sign said 57 miles to Tampa.

Q16: He exhaled a puff of smoke.

Q17: Sunshine warmed his bones.

Q18: Waiting for change, the woman adjusted her belt and brushed her hair.

Q19: I move my feet so he can sit on the cot facing the blue screen and get to it.

Q20: The man pushed some buttons and stared at the screen.

Q21: Each day at 11:55, the elderly widower walked to the center of the hamlet and waited at the pedestrian crossing.

Q22: After standing there a few minutes, the old man would go home.

Q23: While drinking coffee on a terrace, I heard terrible barking.

Q24: Sabra thought about the evening.

Q25: He ate breakfast, then dragged his wife through town, pointing out the sights.

Q26: His wife saw the setting sun.

Q27: I sashayed across the room.

Q28: The three twisted, spun, somersaulted to the blanket.

Q29: I read in a magazine of an American who took one Polaroid photo each day in his life. We added the word photo to add more clarity to the sentence.

Q30: The party really was miserable.

Q31: Several ways to do this. Here's ours: Since I left New York, I miss lobsters.

Q32: Moments later, Sam screamed.

Q33: Ronald was tall, dark, handsome, rich, brilliant.

Q34: Harry ate strange-looking food aliens gave him.

Q35: We stood at the edge of Martian helium pools.

Q36: They said she was dead, but he knew they were lying.

Q37: The gift cost $5.77. We cut *with tax*, because it's a superfluous detail.

# CHAPTER 8: DEVELOPING MINIMALIST NARRATIVE – PART 2

This chapter discusses how to meet minimalist objectives when developing narrative in your drabbles.

- **"Beginning To"**
- **Logic Errors**
- **Transitions**
- **Telling Then Correcting**
- **Passive to Active**
- **"There" or "It"**
- **Character Motives**
- **Cryptic Sentences**
- **Obscure Words**

Let's look at the first topic…

**"BEGINNING TO"**

If somebody is starting or beginning to do something, they're already doing it. Also, you can save WC by just telling us what they were doing and omitting *was starting to* or *was beginning to*. Do this by converting the verb to past tense. Here are some examples:

BEFORE: *Jan was starting to protest.*
AFTER: *Jan protested.*
BEFORE WC: 5
AFTER WC: 2
GAINED WC: 3

BEFORE: *He was beginning to get a headache.*
AFTER: *He got a headache.*
BEFORE WC: 7
AFTER WC: 4
GAINED WC: 3

Q1: Rewrite the sentence: *She started noticing that I was always forgetting where I put my keys.*

Q2: Fix this sentence*: Joe's face started getting red.*

Q3: Rewrite this sentence: *Linda's eyes started to widen; her mouth started to form an O.*

Q4: *Charlie began to regret this weekend as soon as she'd called for him.*

Q5: What two reasons did we give for rewriting sentences that tell us characters are starting to do something in a scene?

## LOGIC ERRORS

Logic errors in drabbles annoy readers and can waste word count. For example, we've seen stories in which a character walks into a dark room, but somehow can see everything within the room.

Here's another example: *The flower girl walked down the aisle spreading rose petals, while bridesmaids walked slowly up the aisle.*

Q6: Identify the logic error in the sentence above.

Another example: *The flowers stood in assembly as if they'd suddenly become self-conscious of the boy staring at them.*

Attributing self-consciousness to flowers doesn't make sense, unless the story's a fantasy tale. However the story in which this sentence appeared wasn't a work of fantasy.

Look at this one: *It's a similar yet different kind of thing with others who are no longer here.*

Q7: What's the logic error in the sentence above?

Another example: *"Where are we?" Fred asked. Joan opened her mouth as if to reply, but the look on Fred's face showed that he did not like the answer.*

The error here is that the female character didn't say anything, but the male didn't like the answer she didn't give. How can anyone know he doesn't like an answer, if one hasn't been given? Note also that the second sentence uses 22 words, or almost one fourth of the drabble.

Q8: What's the logic error in this sentence? *The crowd answers with silence.*

Remember to examine your manuscripts to ensure you haven't wasted WC on illogical statements. Including them may distract editors and throw them out of the story.

## TRANSITIONS

Ensure your transitions from one scene or event to another use as few words as possible. This is often a stumbling block for authors. Here are some ways to overcome this potential problem. Let's look at the two opening sentences of our drabble that won first prize in a contest.

### TASTY SNACKS

*Frank wondered if the cannibalistic Three Moons Tribe really existed. He headed to Peru to investigate.*

Notice how fast we got Frank to Peru. We could've said *he went to the airport, boarded a wide-bodied plane and headed for Peru to investigate,* but that would've expended too much WC. We thought it wasn't vital to explain exactly how he got there. Readers know from experience that characters usually fly when traveling long distances. We relied on that knowledge to cut the WC.

The next two sentences were:

*Knocked unconscious in the jungle, he woke inside a pot. A fire blazed underneath.*

Notice how quickly we got him into the jungle where something extremely unpleasant happened. We could've included a cookbook procedure to explain how he got from, say, his plane to the jungle, such as: *Reaching Peru, he left the plane, rented a car at the airport, and drove 200 miles to the jungle.* That would've expended too much WC. By placing him in the jungle, readers will assume he got there somehow. Exactly how that happened isn't vital to the plot. The story isn't about how he got from one point to another—it's about his investigation.

We also avoided excessive WC by not describing the event of meeting the tribesmen. Instead we said he was knocked unconscious, and even worse, he ended up in a pot. This builds an image to readers that he must've encountered the tribe he was seeking. Finding himself in a pot with a blazing fire underneath seems to confirm he met the tribesmen he was seeking, and they are cannibals.

At this point, we used only 30 WC. 70 more remained to tell the rest of the story.

When we make quick transitions such as these, we avoid spoon-feeding information to readers. We rely on them to fill in the blanks. This contrasts with novels and short stories in which transitions are often more detailed.

The ability to make minimalist transitions is one of the keys to telling as much story as possible in as few words as possible.

If you're wondering what happened to Frank, we'll examine this drabble in greater detail in Chapter 9: Anatomy of a Prize-Winning Drabble.

## TELLING THEN CORRECTING

One way to waste WC in drabbles is to tell something, then immediately correct it. Example: *Lisa brought me some new clothes. Well, they aren't new, but who needs new?*

By changing *new* in the first sentence to *used*, the second sentence could be deleted.

BEFORE: *Lisa brought me some new clothes. Well, they aren't new, but who needs new?*
AFTER: *Lisa brought me some used clothes.*
BEFORE WC: 14
AFTER WC: 6
GAINEDWC: 8

Another example: *Her parents were dead. Not just dead; they'd been torn apart, their limbs strewn around the room.*

We think it would've been enough to tell us: *Her parents' body parts were scattered around the room.* If their body parts were scattered, we can assume they were dead. Further, scattered body parts gives the idea that the parents had been torn apart, blown apart, or cut into pieces. Let's look at the BEFORE and AFTER:

BEFORE: *Her parents were dead. Not just dead; they'd been torn apart, their limbs strewn around the room.*
AFTER: *Her parents' body parts were scattered around the room.*
BEFORE WC: 17
AFTER WC: 9
GAINED WC: 8

Here's another example: *Mark felt stranded in the middle of nowhere. Not exactly stranded, since his car was in good working order and remained parked exactly where he had left it; and not exactly the middle of nowhere, since he had followed accurate directions to get there.*

In this case, the author wasted WC by correcting himself twice. This could've been avoided with more careful thought about how to describe the character's situation.

Look at this one: *She couldn't know what I was doing. What Helen and I were doing.* Here's how we can fix this repletion:

BEFORE: *She couldn't know what I was doing. What Helen and I were doing.*
AFTER: *She couldn't know what Helen and I were doing.*
BEFORE WC: 13
AFTER WC: 9
GAINED WC: 4

Another example: *She fixed up a room for me. Well, technically it's a walk-in closet.* We think the author meant: *She made me a room the size of a walk-in closet.*

BEFORE: *She fixed up a room for me. Well, technically it's a walk-in closet.*
AFTER: *She made me a room the size of a walk-in closet.*
BEFORE WC: 13
AFTER WC: 11
GAINED WC: 2

Another example: *It's Monday and today I'm wearing crystal balls. That is, crystal ball earrings.*

The second sentence can be deleted by rewriting the first one: *It's Monday and I'm wearing crystal ball earrings.* Note that we cut the word *today* from the first sentence. If it's Monday, then the word *today* is assumed because the sentence is written in present tense.

BEFORE: *It's Monday and today I'm wearing crystal balls. That is, crystal ball earrings.*
AFTER: *It's Monday and I'm wearing crystal ball earrings.*
BEFORE WC: 13
AFTER WC: 8
GAINED WC: 5

Look at this example: *I had no choice. No, that's not true, but I didn't realize it wasn't.* How would you handle this, considering the two sentences contain five negative words: *no, No, not, didn't wasn't?*

Here are more examples:

- *I breathed longly, or longingly, I'm not sure which.*
- *Her face was blank. No, not blank; puzzled slightly, a bit afraid, maybe, but not blank.*
- *She realized that he had been staring at a blank screen. A blank blue screen.*

Q9: Fix this sentence to preserve the idea and eliminate needless words. HINT: try two sentences. *As the thing lurches upright, I can see now that it is an old woman with snake eyes...a dead old woman with snake eyes and peeling flesh.*

Remember: you should always remain in control of your narrative sentences. Don't make statements, then waste words to correct them.

## PASSIVE TO ACTIVE

Sentences written in passive mode usually expend more words than when they're written in active mode. Here's an example:

BEFORE: *Fred was given a solid handshake by the chief.*
AFTER: *The chief gave Fred a solid handshake.*
BEFORE WC: 9
AFTER WC: 7
GAINED WC: 2

In this case, switching from passive voice to active cuts two WC.

Q10: Fix this sentence: *Fred was abducted by aliens.*

## "THERE" OR "IT"

Some sentences that begin with *There* or *It* are often weaker than necessary. Further, a simple rewrite of the sentences allows you to cut words.

Here's an example: *There in the dirt squatted a man.*

By reversing the word sequence, *There* can be eliminated: *A man squatted in the dirt.*

Here are more examples:

BEFORE: *There were three girls there.*
AFTER: *Three girls were there.*
BEFORE WC: 5
AFTER WC: 4
GAINED WC: 1

BEFORE: *There have been missionaries from other religions to drop by now and then.*
AFTER: *Missionaries from other religions drop by now and then.*
BEFORE WC: 13
AFTER WC: 9
GAINED WC: 4

BEFORE: *There were hundreds of birds inside my room.*
AFTER: *Hundreds of birds were inside my room.*
BEFORE WC: 8
AFTER WC: 7
GAINED WC: 1

Q11: Fix this sentence: *There were ten zombies running toward me.*

Q12: Rewrite this sentence: *There was a curious smell in the air.*

Q13: Fix this sentence: *There was a photograph of Mary on the screen.*

The same problem sometimes occurs with *It*. Here's an example: *It was the bar nearest their station that was still open.*

Q14: Rewrite this: *It was the bar nearest their station that was still open.*

Q15: Cut words without changing the meaning: *It was a routine that saved Joe's life time and time again.*

Q16: What two reasons did we give to avoid starting a sentence in drabbles with *There* or *It ?*

## CHARACTER MOTIVES

We've seen drabbles in which character's motives are questioned, but not answered. We think authors shouldn't waste words on this kind of speculation.

Here's an example: *Whether out of some hidden altruistic streak or because the aliens were taking away her food supply, Lisa cursed at the sight.*

We think authors should know everything about drabbles they write. Thus, they shouldn't waste words speculating about questions that can't be answered. Here's how we'd rewrite the sentence:

BEFORE: *Whether out of some hidden altruistic streak or because the aliens were taking away her food supply, Lisa cursed at the sight.*
AFTER: *Lisa cursed when aliens removed her food supply.*
BEFORE WC: 22

AFTER WC: 8
GAINED WC: 14

Here's another example: *"Your wife should get a job." Harry wasn't sure if his dad spoke out of love or hate.*

We'd delete the second sentence, because there's no way to answer this question, unless Harry asks his dad if he's speaking out of love or hate.

Q17: Fix this sentence: *"Yeah. Fine." He looked around, as if remembering.*


## CRYPTIC SENTENCES

When reviewing and writing formal critiques for drabbles, we often found ourselves asking, "What does that mean?" Here's an example: *She squints against the medicinal white light.*

We were thrown out of the story when we paused to consider how medicinal white light might be different from white light coming from a bulb in a desk lamp. We never found out, because the story didn't tell us. The story wasn't set in a medical facility so we wondered why the author chose the adjective *medicinal.* The entire sentence should've been deleted because it gave a trivial detail about what she did with her eyes.

More examples:

- *He worked the shallow end of the gene pool.*
- *It back-flipped a parachute-like maneuver involving...*
- *She chewed on the air as she swam into the crowd.*
- *He smashed the statue until it was a scattered conference of bothered paper.*

- *No way out, his footsteps told him.*
- *Candy corn is forever.*
- *Sometimes the truth has yellow teeth and you hate it when it smiles at you.*
- *The rain drops on the window reflect the somehow familiar sapphire lights that sparkle and dance rhythmically, beating my walls, mesmerizing my senses.*
- *A spoon of honey to your lips, the juiciest gossip you have ever heard but somehow, the secret becomes too sweet for you to handle and the lies and screams at night seem to rot your brain and end up slipping off your tongue every now and then.*

Always strive to make your narrative sentences as clear as possible.

## OBSCURE WORDS

Don't include obscure and rarely used words in your stories, because they may throw editors out of the story.

Here are some examples we've seen in stories:

- *Sibilant*
- *Triptych*
- *Dappled*
- *Flocculent*
- *Grandiloquent*
- *Unctuous*
- *Evanescent*
- *Intaglio*
- *Perambulation*
- *Scudding*

When we saw words like this, we thought the authors were more interested in showing their rich vocabularies than telling a story.

This concludes Chapter 8. The next chapter analyzes a prize-winning drabble to illustrate a number of drabble development techniques covered in this tutorial. We suggest you complete the Word Economy Exercise before reading Chapter 9.

## ANSWERS TO QUESTIONS

Q1: She noticed I kept forgetting where I put my keys.

Q2: Joe's face turned red.

Q3: Linda's eyes widened; her mouth formed an O.

Q4: Charlie regretted this weekend when she called him. We changed the second verb to simple past tense.

Q5: If they are starting to do something or beginning to do something, they are already doing it. Also cuts superfluous words.

Q6: The girl is walking down the aisle, but bridesmaids are walking up the aisle. This gives the idea they are going in different directions and may run into each other. We doubt this is what the author intended.

Q7: A thing can't be similar and different simultaneously. Meanwhile, the sentence is unclear, so we had no idea what the author meant.

Q8: If the crowd is silent, it isn't answering. Thus, it can't answer in silence.

Q9: Several ways to do this. Here's one way: The thing lurches upright. It's a dead old woman with snake eyes and peeling flesh.

Q10: Aliens abducted Fred.

Q11: Ten zombies ran toward me.

Q12: A curious smell was in the air.

Q13: Mary's photograph was on the screen.

Q14: The bar nearest their station was open.

Q15: A routine saved Joe's life repeatedly.

Q16: Makes the sentence sound weaker. Uses more words. Deleting the words *There* or *It* from the beginning of sentences cuts at least 1 WC.

Q17: "Yeah, fine," he said.

# CHAPTER 9: ANATOMY OF A PRIZE-WINNING DRABBLE

This chapter contains one of our drabbles that won First prize in a contest. The story is analyzed in several ways. The purpose is to show how the story was structured to meet minimalist objectives and contest guidelines.

Here's what we'll cover in this discussion:

- **Contest guidelines**
- **What we developed**
- **The drabble that won**
- **Questions on structure and content**
- **Minimalist techniques in the story**
- **Scenes and events**
- **Twist**

## CONTEST GUIDELINES

The guidelines gave this prompt: *three moons*. The drabble had to include those words somewhere in the story. Stories could be any genre. Only one story submission was allowed per author.

## WHAT WE DEVELOPED

We came up with four different ideas. We developed those ideas into four drabbles, all of which met contest guidelines. Here's what we developed:

- An anecdotal crime tale in which a man was murdered. His last words to a friend, who found him, gave a clue: the killer had three moons tattooed on his arm. The friend searched until he found the killer, then took revenge.

- A light sci-fi tale in which three moons suddenly appeared above Earth. Everyone on Earth died from fright thinking the sudden appearance of three moons meant the World was coming to an end. However, the three moons were actually three massive garbage containers Martians were towing to the farthest reaches of the solar system. The Martian garbage men visited Earth, since they were so close. They couldn't understand why they found Earth completely unpopulated.

- An absurdist urban fantasy tale in which a psychiatrist intended to prove once and for all how Earth was created. His method of proof was hypnotic regression. He put a woman into a trance and mentally regressed her. Her mind went back to the point where Earth was created by the collision of three moons. When asked if the moons had names, she gave them: Larry, Curly, and Moe—the names of The Three Stooges.

- An absurdist fantasy tale about a man who wanted to determine if the Three Moons Tribesmen were cannibals. He went to Peru to find out. Instead of telling you the rest of this story idea, you'll see this story in a few moments. It's the one we selected to enter the contest.

Each of these drabbles took about four hours to develop and polish. Since we could submit only one to the contest, we submitted the other three to various magazines. All got accepted and published. The drabble we submitted to the contest won first prize.

## THE DRABBLE THAT WON:

### *TASTY SNACKS*

*Frank wondered if the cannibalistic Three Moons Tribe really existed. He headed to Peru to investigate.*

*Knocked unconscious in the jungle, he woke inside a pot. A fire blazed underneath.*

*"I have herpes, syphilis, leprosy," he hollered. "I'll taste lousy. Besides, cannibalism causes madness and tribal extinction."*

*They didn't understand English.*

*Frank became 30 gallons of chunky soup, 150 patties, 28 pounds of jerky, and 500 sausages. This was sold at tribal-owned, franchised, jungle snack stands.*

*Turns out the Three Moons Tribe aren't cannibals. But the surrounding tribes are.*

*Three Mooners are industrious entrepreneurs, meeting the demands of hungry customers.*

## QUESTIONS ON STRUCTURE AND CONTENT

Now that you've read the entire drabble, ask yourself these questions.

- Did it contain a complete story?
- Did it meet minimalist objectives?
- Did the opener hook you?
- Did the two opening sentences give you an idea of what the story was about?
- Did it achieve word economy in every sentence?
- Was it clearly written?

- Was it free of trivial details?
- Did it include anything that threw you out of the story?
- Did the story have a protagonist with a goal?
- Did the story have an antagonist?
- Did the story have a twist?
- Did the lack of a last name for the protagonist affect the story?

## MINIMALIST TECHNIQUES IN THE STORY

The drabble is repeated below. This time we've added comments to highlight the minimalist techniques we implemented. Note that cumulative total WC expended is shown in parentheses at various points of the story.

### *TASTY SNACKS*

*Frank wondered if the cannibalistic Three Moons Tribe really existed. He headed to Peru to investigate.* (Cumulative Total WC Expended: 16)

COMMENTS: We used 16 words in two sentences set up the story. Notice the word economy and how tightly this is written.

There's no question what Frank's quest is. Notice how quickly we got him to Peru. We could've said *he boarded a plane or ship and headed for Peru.* But that would've burned up excessive WC. We thought it not vital to the plot to explain how he got there. Readers know from experience that characters use airliners for long distance travel.

Note also that we didn't give Frank a last name. There's no point wasting WC on a last name readers won't care about. We've read countless drabbles in which authors wasted words by included the protagonist's last name and repeating it. The only time it's useful to include a last name is when a character is famous or when the last name is used instead of a first.

*Knocked unconscious in the jungle, he woke inside a pot. A fire blazed underneath.* (Cumulative Total WC Expended: 30)

COMMENTS: Notice how quickly we got him into the jungle where something extremely unpleasant happened. We could've included a detailed procedure to explain how he got from, say, his plane to the jungle, such as: *Reaching Peru, he left the plane, rented a car, and drove inland 200 miles to the jungle.* That'd burn up too much WC. By placing him in the jungle immediately, readers will assume he found a way to get there. Exactly how that happened isn't vital to the plot. Remember we had only 100 words to tell a complete story about Frank and his quest to determine if the Three Mooners were cannibalistic.

We also explained what happened to him when he reached the jungle by saying he was knocked unconscious and ended up in a pot. Mentioning a blazing fire underneath, we set up Frank for an unpleasant future. From this, the reader gets the idea that the Three Moons Tribe is indeed cannibalistic. Notice that we didn't say anything about his encounter with them, what they looked like, who knocked him unconscious, or even why they committed a hostile act.

*"I have herpes, syphilis, leprosy," he hollered. "I'll taste lousy. Besides, cannibalism causes madness and tribal extinction."* (Cumulative Total WC Expended: 47)

COMMENTS: We added Frank's dialogue to give a touch of dark humor. We made his statements as crisp as possible. Several rewrites were needed to do this.

*They didn't understand English.* (Cumulative Total WC Expended: 51)

COMMENTS: We put him in a pot, allowed him to say something to try to save himself, but now readers discover his captors didn't understand a word. No doubt he's doomed.

*Frank became 30 gallons of chunky soup, 150 patties, 28 pounds of jerky, and 500 sausages.* (Cumulative Total WC Expended: 67)

COMMENTS: We tried to continue the absurdist dark humor by describing Frank's fate. This gives the impression that the Three Moon Tribe is cannibalistic, and confirms Frank's suspicion.

*This was sold at tribal-owned, franchised, jungle snack stands. Turns out the Three Moons Tribe aren't cannibals. But the surrounding tribes are. Three Mooners are industrious entrepreneurs, meeting the demands of hungry customers.* (Cumulative Total WC Expended: 100.)

COMMENTS: Instead of eating Frank's byproducts, they sold his processed remains at jungle snack stands. We hoped this ludicrous idea and the twist painted a darkly humorous picture. How did you react when reading Frank's fate and the twist?

**SCENES AND EVENTS**

The story has three scenes in which the events occur, followed by a twist.

SCENE-1: *Frank wondered if the cannibalistic Three Moons Tribe really existed. He headed to Peru to investigate.*

Number of Sentences: 2
Number of words: 16
Number of events: 2

- 1st event is the protagonist's mental activity
- 2nd event is his acting on his thought.

Notice we don't know anything about Frank other than what his thought was and that he traveled to Peru. That's because genre drabbles are event-driven, not character driven.

SCENE-2: *Knocked unconscious in the jungle, he woke inside a pot. A fire blazed underneath. "I have herpes, syphilis, leprosy," he hollered. "I'll taste lousy. Besides, cannibalism causes madness and tribal extinction." They didn't understand English.*

Number of Sentences: 6
Number of Words: 35
Number of Events: 3

- 1st event is the protagonist getting knocked unconscious in the jungle.
- 2nd event is his waking and finding himself in a pot that has a fire underneath.
- 3rd event is his talking to his captors.

In drabbles, telling is preferable to showing, because telling uses less WC. However, we can show a bit about the character through dialogue. In this case, we have someone who is probably lying, trying to convince his captors to release him. However, the narrative suggests he's doomed, because they don't understand English.

So far, the only things we know about Frank is that he's inquisitive and will say anything to escape his terrible fate. Also, his words have some truth, because studies indicate cannibalism causes mental derangement, and quite possibly extinction. So, he may be well-educated, but, we'll never know for sure.

SCENE-3: *Frank became 30 gallons of chunky soup, 150 patties, 28 pounds of jerky, and 500 sausages. This was sold at tribal-owned, franchised, jungle snack stands.*

Number of Sentences: 2
Number of Words: 25
Number of Events: 2

- $1^{st}$ event is the transformation of the protagonist into various byproducts.
- $2^{nd}$ event is the sale of the byproducts at jungle snack stands.

Not all genre or anecdotal drabbles consist of so many scenes and events. It's quite common to find one-scene drabbles with one event. You read a one-scene drabble with one event in Chapter 1 that was called, "Home at War's End."

## TWIST

The twist in this story is: *Turns out the Three Moons Tribe aren't cannibals. But the surrounding tribes are. Three Mooners are industrious entrepreneurs, meeting the demands of hungry customers.*

Number of Sentences: 3
Number of Words: 24
Number of Events: 0

Frank was not able to achieve his goal, because his demise prevented it. Thus, the tribesmen were unwitting antagonists who prevented him from discovering the truth.

Here's how we devised the twist. When we were developing this drabble and reached the point where Frank became 30 gallons of chunky soup, 150 patties, 28 pounds of jerky, and 500 sausages, we came to a standstill. We weren't sure what to say next. If we ended the story as we caused readers to expect, it wouldn't have any punch. A guy thinks a tribe is cannibalistic, and now it looks like he's right. That's a mundane result of Frank's inquiry. Mundane stories don't win contests. We wondered how to make the drabble more compelling, considering only 33 WC remained.

After some thought, we got the idea of using an unexpected reversal. We'd often used such reversals in previous stories. We felt we were heading in the right direction when this sentence came to mind: *This was sold at tribal-owned, franchised, jungle snack stands.*

This was the story's turning point, because if they were cannibals, Frank's remains would've been consumed by the Three Mooners. We hoped the contest editor would wonder why they chose to sell the remains. We gave the answer in 24 words: *Turns out the Three Moons Tribe aren't cannibals. But the surrounding tribes are. Three Mooners are industrious entrepreneurs, meeting the demands of hungry customers.*

We spent almost two hours juggling the 24 words of these three sentences. We rewrote, took word counts, rewrote, took word counts, and repeated the same procedure until we got the right combination of words. The effort was worth it, because we created a twist that worked for the contest editor.

This concludes Chapter 9, which is the last chapter of this book. The next page presents a 125-question Word Economy Exercise to give you more practice in achieving minimalist objectives. Answers for the questions appear at the end of the exercise.

# WORD ECONOMY EXERCISE

**The purpose of this exercise is to give you more practice in achieving minimalist objectives. Rewrite each sentence.**

Answers for the 125 questions are presented at the end of this exercise.

Q1: *"What did you say?" I asked, my voice barely above a whisper.*

Q2: *"Go and get me my book," he said.*

Q3: *Bobby drove his sparkling Mercedes that his housekeeper just waxed, to the spa.*

Q4: *I figured it would take me an hour to critique his story.*

Q5: *He was able to reel himself and his wild instincts in.*

Q6: *I knew that everyone had wifi broadband these days.*

Q7: *Jane spotted several campfires in a clearing made by a construction crew earlier in the year.*

Q8: *It was the first amount of alcohol that had passed his lips since he could remember.*

Q9: *A trickle of sweat began to run down his cheek.*

Q10: *Harry's anxieties, which he had been keeping at bay, suddenly overwhelmed his senses.*

Q11: *The movement created a stench that hitched a ride to her nose.*

Q12: *Claire raised her hand, trying to brush away the memories, she had tried so hard over the years to forget.*

Q13: *He lifted his gray head and with stiff, cracked fingers, thrust a frayed brown hat at me.*

Q14: *A well-dressed woman, pearls glittering at her throat, passed by.*

Q15: *His dour songs remind me of the splinters in the floorboards of the old house, the one he left us in when he walked off, walked out, walked away.*

Q16: *Every night Jason would walk through the park, that old song would play over and over in his head.*

Q17: *He had carved their initials on a tree with a heart around them.*

Q18: *The cop met Detective Kelly at the door to the motel room.*

Q19: *She had her hands folded across her chest, and she was glaring across the room at him.*

Q20: *Harry went over to look at the body.*

Q21: *He sat back and blessed her with his smile again.*

Q22: *Rob stretched his lean body with exaggeration and faced his brother.*

Q23: *Still in a high state of excitement, Mary seemed unconcerned that she was staring into the barrel of her own gun.*

Q24: *He reached over to a vase of flowers on the kitchen table, breathed on them, and they wilted instantly.*

Q25: *Ashley sat next to him at the table, and held his hands. They were very cold.*

Q26: *There were lines of sorrow around her eyes and mouth, but there was no denying that she was beautiful.*

Q27: *But, instead of complaining as I had every right to do, I let it go with a sigh.*

Q28: *The transit cops had a nasty habit of not allowing him on the train when he was armed.*

Q29: *She spoke a Creole that the tourists and even the locals experienced difficulty understanding.*

Q30: *The waitress had been the mellow kind, our favorite, so she hadn't bothered to ask for i.d.'s when we ordered drinks.*

Q31: *Charlie wasn't shooting off his leering grin for a change.*

Q32: *Erica stretched out a finger and touched the boy's icy cheek.*

Q33: *Sally realized something was wrong and let out a piercing scream.*

Q34: *Suffice it to say this untimely turn of events seriously complicated matters.*

Q35: *The lies fell from his lips and lay discarded on the table next to her lipstick stained napkin.*

Q36: *Even now, she wanted nothing more than to sink into his arms.*

Q37: *Kelly went over to look at the body. It was on the floor, spread-eagled.*

Q38: *"I have need of your talents."*

Q39: *Gary hopped off the hood and started walking off toward the neighborhood.*

Q40: *Erik should have realized that it was going to be a bad day from the moment that he woke up.*

Q41: *Tell the truth, I was pretty thrilled when Sharon answered my question.*

Q42: *I chalked it up to the eccentricities of celebrity.*

Q43: *Angeline rained abuse at him, mocked him.*

Q44: *It slid down her back like water, dark brown water.*

Q45: *I slurped juice from the ceramic spoon that felt too thick and awkward in my mouth.*

Q46: *A sweating face filled Jack's field of vision.*

Q47: *A ball rolled into the street before him, followed by a pink-faced moppet of a girl sprinting after it.*

Q48: *Lloyd slams on the brakes and has his window rolled down before the screeching tires can finish sending their echo through the tall oaks that line the sidewalk.*

Q49: *She pulled over to the shoulder and watched in the side mirror as the officer approached her car.*

Q50: *Tearing the envelope across the top with the letter opener, she withdrew it.*

Q51: *The highway was empty. Not another car ahead or behind.*

Q52: *There was a badge pinned over his left shirt pocket.*

Q53: *She sat more than halfway back in the rail car.*

Q54: *She came closer, and I caught a whiff of her perfume.*

Q55: *I smelled the incense as the breeze blew in my direction.*

Q56: *Chad picked up his cell phone to check the time on its luminous display.*

Q57: *Not four feet in front of his eyes, a girl dressed in a long gingham skirt, ruffled white blouse and apron stirred sizzling chunks of meat and peppers around in a kettle.*

Q58: *The young woman twisted to look out the window carved into the opposite wall.*

Q59: *The metallic clang of the spoon she dropped seemed to echo into the crescendo of the approaching hoof beats.*

Q60: *The ground was damp beneath her skirts.*

Q61: *Wish I could remember where I put the batteries – ditto for the candles.*

Q62: *Men gushed with envious stares as dad whirled his dark-haired beauty around the dance floor.*

Q63: *He picked up the grainy photograph and looked at it.*

Q64: *Harry paid his bill, left a tip, then walked out to his car.*

Q65: *He sort of expected something like this to happen at some point.*

Q66: *The numerous reporters gathered around the podium.*

Q67: *Benjamin crinkled his brow and hissed, "Shut up, Bet!"*

Q68: *She paid no attention to him at all.*

Q69: *He gave her a cocky, full-of-himself, smile.*

Q70: *She extended her index finger on her free hand, and motioned for him to sit back down.*

Q71: *Linda poured the bourbon into two glasses.*

Q72: *Tom gasped, clutched his chest and fell to the floor.*

Q73: *The werewolf invited me to take a seat with him.*

Q74: *A frown settled onto her face.*

Q75: *"Are you sure?" she questioned with a wrinkle of disappointment growing in her forehead.*

Q76: *"Wait, I've got an umbrella," she cried and reached into the beach bag she was carrying and pulled out a very large black umbrella.*

Q77: *"My name's Megan," she announced extending her small hand to him.*

Q78: *"Well she said she would be right back," Evan started to explain.*

Q79: *"Oh yeah, a big difference," she laid heavy emphasis on the word big and began to nod some more.*

Q80: *The rain overhead started to slow down.*

Q81: *They are in opposition to a quick settlement.*

Q82: *"My name is Joe," he introduced to the girl.*

Q83: *That afternoon, Harry was awarded the first prize.*

Q84. *"What's your project?" the Universal Science Fair judge asked.*

Q85: *They dumped the experiment in the trash then went inside to play video games.*

Q86: *He had a gloating look on his face.*

Q87: *I just couldn't figure it out.*

Q88: *I screamed as I saw him gnashing through the bars of the cage that separated us.*

Q89: *She wore concern in the shape of her lips and the arch of her eyebrows.*

Q90: *Gary brought the car to a stop and rolled down the window.*

Q91: *Clenching my teeth, I looked toward the closed bedroom door of my new roommate.*

Q92: Ed *popped the last bite of his burger into his mouth.*

Q93: *While walking down the street, he passed by a white van.*

Q94: *A little after five a battered F-150 pulled up, and there was Eula as I remembered her: work boots, heavy canvas shorts, a worn T-shirt, and sweat-stained ball-cap.*

Q95: *We drove out to the forest.*

Q96: *The next day, I was unable to track Nora down.*

Q97: *Anytime I got in touch with my friend, I'd ask if he'd seen Charlie.*

Q98: *He used all the weapons at his disposal, but nothing seemed to work.*

Q99: *We cooked up some steaks over an open fire.*

Q100: *She snarled as the pain and hunger consumed her.*

Q101: *He turned, sighed, and then opened the front door.*

Q102: *Make your writing as clear as possible at all times.*

Q103: *I picked up the phone and called room service, ordered the pizza without question, in an almost normal voice.*

Q104: *He sashayed in, in that way of his.*

Q105: *I took a bow and went back to my seat.*

Q106: *"Tell me about that future of mine."*

Q107: *I had not much money.*

Q108: *He has taken in his mind to sell the house.*

Q109: *Her husband, Joe, had died years ago, not to mention her own parents before that and one of her children, a son.*

Q110: *Andrew did not submit his management report that month and was summarily let go*

Q111: *Why did Mom and Dad give all his things away, all his toys, all his clothes, all his furniture, even his bicycle?*

Q112: *"It is fear that is at the root of all of your indecision."*

Q113: *I wondered how much it would cost me to buy a new car.*

Q114: *"I'm not hungry, but you go ahead." I picked at the ice around my mug and took a sip.*

Q115: *"I'll keep a few music CDs and books," he said drily, as he looked at the tree shedding yellow flowers in the garden*

Q116: *After a while they all fell silent and turned their faces to the clock.*

Q117: *Mrs Charlene Smith bristled somewhat, flicked some dust off her skirt and curtly said, "Who asked me that silly question?"*

Q118: *"You folks want something to drink?" The waitress dropped off menus and flicked her Zippo several times before lighting the candle at center table.*

Q119: *So there I was, up on stage, in front of hundreds and hundreds of laughing spectators.*

Q120: *It was like she wanted to show him how much she cared for him, so she baked him a cake.*

Q121: *When I was a child, my father said I pried into the crevices of other people's lives.*

Q122: *In truth, I didn't take part in much of those discussions.*

Q123: *"I can wait," the lady said placing a copy of the Daily Mail on the plush purple chair before sitting down on it then pulling out a copy of Homes and Gardens.*

Q124: Susan stepped into the house.

Q125: A few days ago, I forget which one, I even felt too weak to shave.

# ANSWERS FOR WORD ECONOMY EXERCISE

Q1: "What did you say?" I asked.

Q2: "Get my book," he said.

Q3: Bobby drove his Mercedes to the spa.

Q4: I figured it'd take an hour to critique his story.

Q5: He controlled himself.

Q6: Everyone had wifi broadband.

Q7: Jane spotted several campfires in a clearing.

Q8: It was his first alcoholic drink in a long time.

Q9: Sweat ran down his cheek.

Q10: Harry's suppressed anxieties overwhelmed him. (At bay = suppressed.)

Q11: The movement created a stench.

Q12: Clair tried to forget bad memories.

Q13: He thrust a frayed brown hat at me.

Q14: A well-dressed woman wearing pearls passed by.

Q15: His dour song remind me that he deserted us.

Q16: Every night Jason walked through the park, an old song would repeat in his head.

Q17: He'd carved a heart and their initials on a tree.

Q18: The cop met Detective Kelly at the motel room door.

Q19: Hands folded across her chest, she glared at him.

Q20: Harry looked at the body.

Q21: He smiled at her again.

Q22: Rob faced his brother.

Q23: Though highly excited, Mary seemed unconcerned that she was staring into the barrel of her own gun.

Q24: When he breathed on flowers on the kitchen table, they wilted instantly.

Q25: Ashley sat next to him and held his cold hands. Combining into one sentence saves WC.

Q26: Lines of sorrow surrounded her eyes and mouth, but she was beautiful.

Q27: I didn't complain.

Q28. Transit cops didn't allow him on the train when he was armed.

Q29: She spoke a Creole that tourists and locals couldn't understand.

Q30: The waitress didn't ask for id's when we ordered drinks.

Q31: Charlie wasn't grinning for a change.

Q32: Erica touched the boy's icy cheek.

Q33: Sally realized something was wrong and screamed.

Q34: This untimely event seriously complicated matters.

Q35: He lied.

Q36: She wanted to embrace him.

Q37: Kelly saw the body spread-eagled on the floor.

Q38: "I need your talents."

Q39: Gary hopped off the hood and walked toward the neighborhood.

Q40: Erik should've realized it was gonna be a bad day when he woke up.

Q41: I was thrilled when Sharon answered my question.

Q42: I considered it an eccentricity of celebrity.

Q43: Angeline abused and mocked him.

Q44: It slid down her back.

Q45: I slurped juice from the ceramic spoon.

Q46: Jack saw a sweating face.

Q47: A girl chased a ball down the street.

Q48: Lloyd slams the brakes and quickly rolls down the window.

Q49: She pulled over to the shoulder and waited for the officer.

Q50: She removed the letter from the envelope.

Q51: The highway was empty. Second sentence deleted, because empty means no cars ahead or behind.

Q52: Several ways to do this. Here's our way: He wore a badge.

Q53: She sat in the rail car.

Q54: When she came closer, I smelled her perfume.

Q55: I smelled incense.

Q56: Chad checked the time on his cell phone.

Q57: A girl stirred food in a kettle.

Q58: The young woman looked out the window.

Q59: She dropped a spoon when she heard hoofbeats.

Q60: The ground was damp.

Q61: Wish I could remember where I put the batteries and candles.

Q62: Men stared enviously as dad danced with his dark-haired beauty.

Q63: He looked at the grainy photograph.

Q64: Harry paid his bill, left a tip, went to his car.

Q65: He expected something like this to happen, eventually.

Q66: Numerous reporters gathered around the podium.

Q67: Benjamin said, "Shut up, Bet!"

Q68: She paid no attention to him.

Q69: He smiled at her.

Q70: "Sit down," she said. (We changed the narrative to dialogue to cut WC.)

Q71: Linda poured bourbon into two glasses.

Q72: Tom gasped, clutched his chest, collapsed.

Q73: The werewolf invited me to sit.

Q74: She frowned.

Q75: "Are you sure?" she asked.

Q76: "Wait, I've got an umbrella." She pulled one from her beach bag.

Q77: "I'm Megan." She offered her hand.

Q78: "Well, she said she'd be right back," Evan said.

Q79: "Oh yeah, a big difference," she said.

Q80: The rain slowed.

Q81: They're opposed to a quick settlement.

Q82: "My name's Joe," he told the girl.

Q83: Harry won first prize that afternoon.

Q84. "What's your project?" the judge asked.

Q85: They trashed the experiment, then played video games.

Q86: He gloated.

Q87: I couldn't figure it out.

Q88: I screamed as he gnashed through the bars of the cage.

Q89: She was concerned.

Q90: Gary stopped the car and rolled down the window.

Q91: I looked toward the closed bedroom door of my new roommate.

Q92: Ed ate the rest of his burger.

Q93: Walking down the street, he passed a white van.

Q94: Eula arrived in a truck a little after 5:00, wearing work clothes.

Q95: We drove to the forest.

Q96: The next day, I couldn't find Nora.

Q97: Whenever I contacted my friend, I'd ask if he'd seen Charlie.

Q98: None of his weapons worked.

Q99: We cooked steaks over an open fire. .

Q100: She snarled as pain and hunger consumed her.

Q101: He opened the front door.

Q102: Always write clearly.

Q103: I called room service and ordered pizza.

Q104: He sashayed in.

Q105: I bowed and returned to my seat.

Q106: "Tell me my future."

Q107: I had little money.

Q108: He's decided to sell the house.

Q109: Her husband, parents, and son had died years ago.

Q110: Andrew was fired for not submitting his management report that month.

Q111: Why did Mom and Dad gave away his toys, clothes, furniture, bicycle?

Q112: Fear is the root of all your indecision.

Q113: I wondered how much a new car cost.

Q114: "I'm not hungry, but you go ahead."

Q115: "I'll keep a few music CDs and books," he said.

Q116: After a while they fell silent and looked at the clock.

Q117: Mrs. Smith said, "Who asked me that silly question?"

Q118: "You folks want something to drink?" asked the waitress.

Q119: I was on stage in front of hundreds of laughing spectators.

Q120: She baked a cake for him to show how much she cared.

Q121: When I was a child, my father said I pried into other peoples' lives.

Q122: I didn't take part in much of those discussions.

Q123: "I can't wait," the lady said.
Q124: Susan entered the house.
Q125: A few days ago, I felt too weak to shave.

# BOOKS BY MICHAEL A KECHULA

The Area 51 Option
A Full Deck of Zombies
I Never Kissed Judy Garland
Martians, Monsters and Peperoni Pizza
Micro Fiction: Writing 100 Word Stories
Writing Genre Flash Fiction the Minimalist Way

Printed in Great Britain
by Amazon.co.uk, Ltd.,
Marston Gate.